W9-AGJ-334

*S*pirits
Between the Bays
Series

Volume III

Welcome Inn

Haunted inns,
restaurants,
and museums

by Ed Okonowicz

*M*yst and *L*ace Publishers

Spirits Between the Bays
Volume III
Welcome Inn
First Edition
Copyright 1995 by Edward M. Okonowicz Jr.
All rights reserved.

ISBN 0-9643244-4-X

Published by
Myst and Lace Publishers
1386 Fair Hill Lane
Elkton, Maryland 21921

Printed in the U.S.A.
by Modern Press

Typography and Design
by Kathleen Okonowicz

Dedications

To Diane, Connie and Monica,
Thanks for the memories
that only we can share.
Ed Okonowicz

To my sister, Eileen,
For the best times,
the lost time
and the time yet to come.
Kathleen Burgoon Okonowicz

Acknowledgments

The author and illustrator appreciate the assistance of those
who have played an important role in this project.

Special thanks are extended to:

Kathlene Stegura
for her technical expertise

and

John Brennan
Sue Moncure,
Ted Stegura
and
Monica Witkowski
for their proofreading and suggestions.

Table of Contents

Legend and Lore

Introduction

What is a tracker of phantoms to do?

To what place can an aspiring ghost hunter go?

Where does a seeker of spirits start the search?

How does the prying person with curious cat characteristics gain entree into the underworld of phantoms and specters and things that go bump in the night?

Since many ghosts reside in private homes—and ghost books rarely reveal the exact addresses or the names of current owners of haunted houses—it's difficult to get started in the ghost hunting business.

Welcome Inn offers information that may be used to solve this occupational difficulty.

The stories in this volume of the **Spirits Between the Bays** series have been selected so that readers—who range from the mildly curious to the actively enthusiastic—will be able to go to these sites and actually tour a possessed museum, stay overnight in an inn's haunted room or dine in a restaurant that has entertained those who tend to float in without making a reservation.

These buildings, which serve as hosts for the ghosts, vary in age, size, structure and purpose.

There is Fort Delaware, a weathered Civil War prison on an island; Wilmington's Rockwood Museum, a preserved country estate; the Chadds Ford Inn, once a stopping place for travelers; Dover's Blue Coat Inn, a popular eatery; and, of course, several Eastern Shore bed and breakfast inns. At all of these well-known and historic properties, the spirits of former owners or passing visitors have decided to remain.

1

But, more importantly, they also seem willing to make their presence known.

Early on in our ghostly investigations of museums, historic restaurants and country inns, we discovered that it was quite common for spirits to be referred to by name.

Current owners and on-site managers speak quite casually about "J.J." or "Alexander," "Katie" or "Joseph," "John" or "Margaret." Also, several ghost hosts admit that they have developed a unique bond—involving elements of trust, understanding, respect and friendship—with their elusive and reclusive guests.

Therefore, visitors should tread carefully, for some protectors of the phantoms have become quite possessive about their mysterious friends.

Nevertheless, all of the current owners and caretakers of the haunted sites in this volume have given their permission to share their stories in this book.

In fact, several ghost keepers said they are quite willing to discuss their encounters, to point out the "hot" spots where their building's phantoms have appeared, and to proudly introduce visiting spirit searchers to the resident spooks . . . as long as the restless wanderers happen to be receptive to receiving guests at that particular time.

But novices should heed this advice:

Nothing is ever certain in the ghost business. Independent spirits no longer follow a schedule, punch a time clock, accept personal responsibility for their actions or respond to the whims of demanding bosses or irritating kinfolk.

Ghosts appear when they alone decide to make their presence known.

Manifestations may depend upon a phantom's preference, mood, whim and, of course, the disposition and sensitivity of the seeker.

The well-known phrase "being at the right place at the right time" has never been more appropriate than in ghost hunting.

For those desperately seeking Casper, creaks and bumps can become thumping footsteps, the wind is a howling moan, twigs tapping against a window can be perceived as a bad omen, a frigid draft could be a passing, unseen entity . . . and total silence on a dark and foggy night might actually be a warning of the stillness before the storm.

One must learn to be patient and not allow eagerness and desire to affect solid reasoning and sound judgment.

To readers who decide to go in search of the unseen: *Good luck and Godspeed.*

Until we meet again, six months from now, in **Possessed Possessions: Haunted Antiques, Furniture and Collectibles.**

Happy hauntings, and don't forget your rosary and holy water.

—Ed Okonowicz,
in Fair Hill, Maryland,
at the northern edge of
the Delmarva Peninsula
Fall 1995

Afterthoughts:

As one can imagine, the number of public haunted sites we have discovered exceeded the limited space available in the pages of **Welcome Inn**.

But, those who enjoy the spirit of the chase should rest easy. An upcoming volume of the **Spirits** series will feature more haunted public places. We consider this a special service that will help our readers continue their pursuit of the restless phantoms who leave elusive clues in their purposeful effort to entice us toward the odd, the unusual, the bizarre and the unexplained.

•In the Spring of 1996, Myst and Lace Publishers will present a unique collection of bizarre experiences involving everyday objects in **Possessed Possessions: Haunted Antiques, Furniture and Collectibles**

•The **Spirits Between the Bays** series continues in the Fall of 1996 with the release of **In the Vestibule**. That volume will feature more true ghost tales of the Delmarva Peninsula.

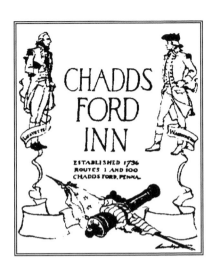

Permanent Residents of the Chadds Ford Inn

One can only imagine the number of travelers—both notables and ne'er do wells—who have passed by the wide, wooden porch of the Chadds Ford Inn, now a Colonial-era restaurant located along U.S. Route 1 on the well-used, centuries-old direct route between Philadelphia and Baltimore.

While many travelers lodged at the inn during the years it operated as a hostelry, there are, it seems, several guests who have decided to stay well past the traditional check-out time. Even though the inn now operates strictly as a restaurant and bar, these secretive stragglers have decided that it is their right to remain.

Apparently, the arrangements are agreeable to all concerned—that being the owners, workers and reclusive residents.

Heavens knows, these usually unseen guests do not take up any space, they never register any complaints about the accommodations or service, and they do not run up a bar tab.

How could they?

They are ghosts.

Whether it's Katie, who seems to command the front of the building; Simon, who operates primarily in the back kitchen area; the grizzled sea captain who has laid claim to his favorite table, and the little boy who roams about on the second floor; or the floating lady, gowned in white garments who wanders downstairs—all have made themselves a home at the Chadds Ford Inn, and they seem to be there to stay.

Jeffrey Theodore now owns the inn, and his late mother, Dorothy, ran it before him. But the structure's legacy as a traveler's haven can be traced almost to its very beginnings, in the early days of the 18th century.

It was in 1703 when Francis Chadsey, an English Quaker from Wiltshire, purchased 500 acres of choice land from William Penn's commissioner for land grants and built his home that is now known as the Chadds Ford Inn.

In 1717, Chadsey's eldest son, John Chad (as the younger man signed his name), took over the estate and ran the family ferry that crossed the Brandywine Creek. In 1736, he turned his father's house into a tavern, and, from far and near, travelers would shout that they would meet at "the tavern at Chad's fording place."

Thus began the long and distinguished legacy of the impressive landmark that dominates the busy highway running through the center of Chadds Ford, Pennsylvania.

But when the ragged logs were still fresh, and the soil in the cellar was damp from the hand-dug excavation, the building was an outpost in a region that was uninhabited, unspoiled and unknown.

During the early years of the American Revolution, fate selected the Brandywine Valley as a site for one of the war's major conflicts. In September 1777, on the rolling meadows, thick woods and rich farmland of southeast Pennsylvania, Gen. George Washington commanded his troops in defeat at the Battle of the Brandywine.

Over the years, Indians passed by on foot, and wagons and carriages carried travelers heading both east and west. Among those using the road were Martha Washington, on her way to spend the winter in Valley Forge, and the Marquis d' Lafayette, during his return trip to the Brandywine battleground in 1825.

Today, numerous antique shops blanket the picturesque valley, and world-famous Longwood Gardens is nearby. The small crossroads town is known throughout the world as the home of three generations of the Wyeths, a family of famous American artists. And other notables, including Howard Pyle and Peter Hurd, who were members of the Brandywine school of American art, lived, worked and studied in the area.

Chadds Ford of the 1990s and the nearby memorial battlefield present an interesting setting, offering a blend of art, culture, history and war in an area where a significant number of soldiers were killed or wounded. Some believe such a tumultuous setting can act as a magnet, attracting wandering souls.

During its 292-year existence, Francis Chadsey's original home has accommodated thousands of travelers and local visitors. Apparently, a few of the patrons were so impressed during their earthly stay that they decided to remain and become informal members of the staff.

✳   ✳   ✳   ✳

When it comes to ghost tales and legends of the Chadds Ford Inn, one must seek out Dawn Jackson.

"Dawn is our ghost specialist," said Joyce, one of the servers, whose assessment was certainly correct.

In an eager, but matter-of-fact tone, Dawn, 36, who grew up in the town and has worked about the inn for nearly 20 years, relayed a series of unusual incidents that she had either witnessed or heard.

"I've never seen anybody," Dawn said, "but I've seen things happen."

Such as faucets turning on, by themselves, in the second-floor bathroom, and water pouring out into the sink—after she had just shut the knobs off.

"It happened to all three of us," she added, referring to her co-workers who were with her at the time.

Then there were the pictures falling off the walls, particularly on the second floor. "It happened when no one was there, and not in heavily traveled areas, either," Dawn said.

In 1986, the inn was preparing to close for renovations, but it wasn't public knowledge at the time. Dawn was working as hostess on a Sunday night. A couple arrived and asked if they could see the second floor, which was not being used that evening.

"When they came down,"Dawn recalled, "one of them told me, 'Whatever you do, don't rearrange the pictures, because you'll upset the spirits.'

"I tell you, I had chills up my spine, and I made sure I told the owner. And I made sure the pictures went back up just the way they were. But I still wonder: *How did they know?*"

One evening a mother, father and daughter arrived. After the father was seated, the two women asked to go upstairs and look around.

"They were only up there a short time," Dawn said, "when they came down and said there was an older person and a very sad and depressed little boy in what we call the Wyeth Room.

"I got the chills again," Dawn said. "I found out they studied ghosts, and they had that sixth sense about them."

Although Dawn has never seen a figure while working at the inn, she recalled the evening, two years ago, when a waiter named Billy received an unusual going away memory.

Billy had been working in the restaurant about eight years, but had given his notice and was planning to move to Hawaii. He had never seen any ghosts, said Dawn, and he didn't believe in their existence.

Near the back stairs on the second floor, he saw a woman in a white dress go into the Board Room. Thinking it was the hostess, he went in to speak to her.

The small dining room was empty.

"He said to me, 'Dawn, it was just as clear as day. I guess I had to see my ghost before I moved to Hawaii.' "

Smiling as she recalled the incident, Dawn said, "He laughed about ghosts all those years. He wasn't afraid to be on the second floor, like a lot of the servers were. He wasn't the type that believed in ghosts, or talked about them a lot. That's why I especially believed what he said."

Another waiter named Bisch, who no longer works at the inn, claimed to have seen a girl in the Hearth Room, to the right of the entrance hall on the main floor. He said she wore a long, flowing white dress and was standing on tiptoes, trying to light a candle on the mantel above the fireplace.

Those who saw Bisch immediately after the sighting said he turned as white as a sheet and didn't move, standing as still as a statue, apparently petrified by what he saw.

Working amidst what may seem to be a bevy of ghostly guests seems to have no negative effect on Dawn.

"I find it extremely interesting, and so do other people," she said. "We do a lot of corporate parties, and I used to take as many as 25 men around in the dark, carrying a lit candle, and give them a tour of the inn. They just loved it, especially when it was raining, thundering and lightning outside.

"I also feel extremely comfortable here," she added. "Part of that is because I do believe that Dorothy Theodore, who was the owner and who passed away about 10 years ago, is here. I knew her when I was in my teens, and I feel like she's my protection when I'm at the inn."

Dawn recalled one other story, this one involving present owner Jeffrey Theodore.

About nine years ago, he was talking excitedly about the renovations he was planning. Standing in the kitchen area, he was describing a few of the details to some of the servers, and then he added, "Boy, if my mother knew what I was going to do, she'd be turning in her grave."

Immediately, Dawn said, a long fluorescent bulb fell out of the ceiling fixture, hit the hard kitchen floor, and rolled. But it didn't break.

While Dawn is one who responds to the unusual in an accepting manner, restaurant manager Anthony Calderaro admitted he has a lower tolerance level for the bizarre.

"Sometimes," Anthony said, "I go around saying, 'I know you're here, but I couldn't handle seeing you.' "

But, Anthony added, both veterans and newcomers on the staff accept the situation well.

"We joke about it." he added. "Some say no way, and others say okay. But everybody agrees that whatever is here is friendly."

Anthony shared the incident that occurred in the Tavern, which is located to the rear of the Brandywine Room and frequented by a group of regulars.

One evening, he said, some of the steady patrons decided to try to stir up some amusement. They called out for Katie the ghost to appear, challenging her to give them a sign if she was really present.

Their taunting hit the jackpot.

The lights suddenly blinked on the computerized cash register and the cash drawer opened by itself and flew back from its casing.

The suddenly silent group slowly dispersed, calling it a night.

The old-fashioned oil lamps in the Tavern will sometimes flare up and glow very brightly without being touched, said Anthony. Also, on a side wall—above the edge of the long, dark wooden bar—is an open shelf where glassware is stored. One evening, Simon the ghost apparently didn't like the bartender, and the spirit kept knocking the glasses off the shelf.

8

Anthony said unusual happenings are not constant, although outsiders may think there is a lot of unexplained activity when all the events that have occurred over the years are summarized.

The Sea Captain is one of the inn's better known spirit world residents. Since his appearances are usually in the same spot—in a chair behind the northeast corner table in the second floor Wyeth Room—the site has been dubbed the "Captain's Table."

One employee, said Anthony, was carrying items up a narrow stairway toward the third floor offices, from the Wyeth Room. As she went up the steps, she felt someone playfully hitting her ankles. Unable to turn in the confined space to see who it was, she yelled for the jokester to stop. But when she got to the top of the stairway and quickly turned . . . no one was there.

"And no one could have gotten away by running down the steps quick enough to disappear or hide," Anthony said.

Gina Crouse has been office manager of the inn for four years.

She laughed as she explained that one of her jobs is to open the building about 6:30 each morning—usually alone—and, often-times, it's still dark.

Her office is on the third floor, and she has seen the results of the spirits' actions in her work area and throughout the building.

"I came in one day, about the crack of dawn," said Gina. "The only other person in the building was the pastry chef, in the kitchen. I immediately smelled a candle being blown out, that distinct scent of sulfur and beeswax."

Gina said she and the chef checked the entire building for over an hour and found no apparent cause.

"I even went into the basement under the bar. It's creepy and I refuse to go down there. But I was worried that something was burning down there and the smell was coming up. I was this far from calling the fire department."

After two hours the smell disappeared.

"We never found the source of it," Gina said. "That was a wierdy."

In Gina's office, on a shelf above her computer, is a heavy, brass carriage clock. On two different occasions, when her boss was in the room with her, the clock moved from the shelf and land-ed on the floor several feet away.

"It made no sound, no crash," she said. "It was like it flew, or floated, out and was moved to the floor. I got upset and said, 'Jeff, did you see that?' He couldn't explain it either."

In November 1994, a group of ghost hunters from the Society for the Investigation of the Unexplained came to the Chadds Ford Inn. They stayed from five in the morning until noon, using video cameras, tape recorders and motion monitors to attempt to catch a ghost.

"I let them in," Gina said. "I was impressed with all their equipment. One was a psychic who used a divining rod. I thought it was really cool."

The group asked for permission to light every candle in the inn, because one of the signs of a haunting is that a spirit will blow a flame out, Gina was told.

She said the psychic with the divining rod walked around the rooms throwing small sugar packets on the floor to mark spots of interest.

After all the members had wandered through the building and completed their surveillance, they met as a group and shared their findings and identified the "hot spots" of ghostly activity.

She said their findings indicated "activity" in the Reception Room and a corner opposite the "Captain's Table" in the Wyeth Room. The third-floor offices were described as "depressed and morose." The searchers also found "indications" on the left side of the mantel in the first-floor Hearth Room.

Gina offered her feelings about working alone in the haunted inn.

"I'm not afraid," she said, "but it does annoy me. They broke my clock. Sometimes I get mad because they waste my time. But it's a power bigger than me. What am I supposed to do? So you live with it."

Although everyone associated with the Chadds Ford Inn has certain feelings about the unusual incidents, Anthony offered his opinion, one that seems to be shared by both the workers and patrons: "I think the situation is kind of neat. There's tons of history that happened in this area, and, apparently, somewhere along the line some of it has stayed."

Chadds Ford Inn
Inn*formation*

Inncidentally: The restaurant is open seven days a week for lunch and dinner. There is a Sunday brunch. Call for reservations. Private dining rooms and catering are available. The inn's menu offers detailed history about the site and the cover illustration (reproduced with permission at the beginning of this story) was originally drawn and signed by Andrew Wyeth.

Innteresting notes: Many artists have signed and personalized the prints that hang throughout the inn. More than 90 percent of the works are by members of the Wyeth family, some no longer available. Original local artwork hangs in the Tavern. Andrew Wyeth has his favorite table, in the northeast corner of the Hearth Room. He is a regular patron who is often accompanied by family members and Helga. Joyce, one of the veteran servers, said for a long time she only knew him as "Andy," and had no idea he was the noted artist.

The Ghost is Inn: Just about everywhere! Hearth Room, Tavern. The "Captain's Table" is in the Wyeth Room. Also the Red Room, Reception Room, Board Room, second-floor bathroom and third-floor offices.

To get Inn touch: The Chadds Ford Inn, Routes 1 and 100, P.O. Box 519, Chadds Ford, PA 19317; telephone (610) 388-7361.

Chapter illustration courtesy of the Chadds Ford Inn

Living in Milford's Parson Thorne Mansion

The Parson Thorne Mansion stands on Silver Hill, in the center of the small town of Milford, which is located on the border of both Kent and Sussex Counties, Delaware. Its weathered brick has an almost pink patina as it absorbs the full brightness of the mid-day sun.

The original part of the large Georgian home—a small one-room, two-story wooden structure—dates back to the 1730s. Additions increased the size, and it served as the main homestead of a large plantation. In the late 1800s, extensive exterior remodeling was done in an apparent attempt to give the Mansion a Victorian appearance.

Still set back from the main thoroughfare of North West Front Street, the building's tall chimneys and sharp peaked roofs dominate the surrounding area. The long driveway cuts through a spacious front lawn that is accented by towering linden trees and mature shrubbery.

The Milford Historical Society has owned and administered the mansion since 1962. Its brochure describes the building as a Southern style of architecture with a large, impressive central portion that is flanked by symmetrical wings.

Today, the structure remains a symbol of a time long past. Residents and tourists cannot help but notice how the Parson Thorne Mansion dramatically contrasts with modern apartment buildings that surround it on three sides.

When the grand building was constructed in the middle of the 18th century, there were spacious fields and vast open country. From its high ground on Silver Hill, one could see the nearby Mispillion River and the comings and goings of merchant ships.

According to the Society's brochure: "The house derives its name from the Rev. Mr. Sydenham Thorne, an Anglican clergyman who arrived in Milford on December 24, 1774, to take charge of Christ Church Mispillion, then located about four miles west of Milford. In 1785, he bought the property and lived there until his death in 1793."

Following Parson Thorne's death, the property was transferred several times, and many of the owners were prominent citizens of the community and the state, including John M. Clayton, who was U.S. Secretary of State under President Zachary Taylor, and Dr. William Burton, Delaware's governor during the early years of the Civil War.

Some former residents and owners are buried in the gray stone walled graveyard at the rear of the property.

James Richard Draper gave the property to the Milford Historical Society. "On Sept. 22, 1962, as part of the celebration of the founding of the town, the house was formally presented to the society at a public ceremony held on the lawn of the house. . . . The Mansion and its grounds have been the scene of numerous festivals and community events."

✳   ✳   ✳   ✳

Susan Jackson Emory, current president of the Milford Historical Society, admitted that society members and tour guides are often asked if the house has ghosts.

"It's something they are always going to ask," she said, seated in the Mansion's attractively restored first-floor parlor. "It's a natural question, given the age of the building. But, none of us who work here, or give the tours, has ever seen anything."

Comfortably, she then focused on subjects she could discuss with authority, in particular, the home itself and some of its interesting furnishings.

Standing in front of the fireplace—which has an iron fireback built by the Deep Creek Furnace in Sussex County before the American Revolution—Susan pointed to Alfreda Wootten—a three-foot-tall, lifelike antique doll.

Susan explained that Alfreda belonged to the granddaughter of Mrs. R. B. Rodebush, a well-known town resident who lived in the Towers, now an inn located in the center of town.

"Apparently, there was not a lot of entertainment in the late 1800s, so she decided to hold a party for her granddaughter,"

And what a party it must have been. The doll was dressed in a wedding gown and, according to a copy of the invitation that still exists, a wedding and reception was held on "Old Christmas Eve" January 5, 1895—with the doll as the bride and a small, live boy as the groom.

Alfreda was given to the Milford Historical Society, and today stands silently in the parlor—her large dark eyes staring across the room, much as she did 100 years ago. She is dressed in her white wedding garb, complete with a lace-topped gown, red velvet sash, white gloves and small flowered veil.

After noticing the thick crown molding and corner cupboards with butterfly shelves flanking the fireplace, one's eyes are drawn to a massive, 8-foot-tall clock. Susan referred to the timepiece, made by W.B. Smith of Milford in 1792, as an important gift. The parlor also hosts a dark colored rectangular, Philadelphia piano (circa 1820), with ornate carvings and spindled legs.

The Mansion's adjacent dining room features both a bull's eye and pier glass mirror, another massive grandfather clock and attractive chairs, set around the large table, bearing seats with needlepoint designs of the Milford town coat of arms.

Stepping down into the kitchen and taking the narrow stairway to the low-ceilinged, second floor of the original wing, one gains a sense of the small size of homes in the 18th century.

Later, standing on the front steps of the mansion, Susan's eyes scanned the town and buildings that now encircle the centuries-old Mansion.

"It's hard to believe that everything around here was nothing but fields and open space at one time," she sighed, "even, in some cases, up to as recently as 30 years ago. Now, the barns and outbuildings are gone, and all we have left is about an acre and a half of the original plantation . . . and the Parson Thorne Mansion."

* * * *

In the fall of 1979, Sande Warren Price moved into the second floor of Parson Thorne Mansion. For $60 a month she was the sole tenant of the expansive home, and had all the privacy anyone could have desired.

The first floor was furnished and open to the public on certain days for tours conducted by the Milford Historical Society. A dark velvet, theater-style rope strung across the bottom of the narrow stairway, indicated to visitors that the second floor—Sande's apartment area—was off limits.

The weather was cool outside when she moved in during the fall. She was pleased with her new quarters, even though the mansion was a bit of a drive to her job near Smyrna, as a clerk at the Bombay Hook Wildlife Preserve.

About two in the morning, soon after she moved in, she was awakened by noises.

"It scared the life out of me," Sande recalled. "Someone was downstairs trying to get into the house."

She immediately called the police, and, as soon as she put down the receiver of the telephone, the whole house filled with music—loud, orchestral music.

"Not singing," Sande stressed, "but it sounded like an entire orchestra was playing. It definitely was not Top 40. But it wasn't funny. I was so scared, I couldn't get my eyes open. Then, I heard the sirens. When I looked out the second floor window, I could see the lights from the police cars coming up the driveway toward the house. There were three of them."

The officers combed the grounds, searching all around the outside and inside of the house.

They didn't find anyone, but one of the officers came away from one of the first floor windows carrying a crowbar. Apparently, whoever was trying to break in must have dropped it as he ran away.

"I didn't want to think about what had just happened," said Sande. "And I didn't tell the police about the music, because they would have thought I was nuts. But, to this day, I think the ghost, or whatever was in the house, created the music to scare the intruder away."

Afterwards, other things started to happen.

Sande heard the sound of footsteps, coming from the attic, above her second-floor apartment. She said whoever or whatever it was would stop and then rustle papers, as if it was searching through files trying to find something. Then, all the sounds would stop.

"At first," she said, "I was scared, because I thought someone might be downstairs or trying to break in. There were several people with keys to the mansion, so I always made sure my deadbolt was latched on my bedroom door. But when I realized it was above me, and probably the ghost, I was actually relieved. I felt safe. I never felt threatened."

Another strange incident that Sande still cannot explain occurred when she returned home one afternoon and discovered grains of sugar poured all over the top of her bedspread. It only happened once, but it was a bit bothersome.

During the Christmas season, she hung a leather strap with sleigh bells on her apartment bedroom door and the bells would shake and jingle in the middle of the night.

"To this day, my mother thinks I was nuts for staying after the night I heard the music," Sande said.

Mother may have known best.

Each night Sande explained that she locked her door from the inside of the bedroom, where there was a wicker rocking chair.

"One morning, I awoke, took a bath and came back into the bedroom and noticed that the rocker was gone. I unlocked the door to the hall—the deadbolt was still latched from inside—and the rocker was standing out on the hall landing. I still get the chills, talking about this after all these years."

At first, she tried to tell herself that she must have moved it for some reason. But, eventually, Sande asked herself: *Why would I have even thought of doing that?*

"I looked around, glanced up at the stairway to the attic, to see if the ghost was looking at me. Then, very slowly, I put the rocker back in my room and it never moved again."

To cope with the antics of her invisible housemate, Sande did what so many others who have lived with a spirit have done: She began talking to it as if it were a friend.

"I used to open the door and shout: 'I'm home!' I never knew if it was a man or a woman, but I felt like it was protecting me."

16

In addition to her day job at Bombay Hook, Sande also worked as a cocktail waitress to earn extra money to go to school. Often, she would get home at two or three in the morning.

One night, she had a feeling someone was following her from the car to the door of the mansion.

"I took a couple of steps and turned. There was a man behind me. I said, 'Hey! What are you doing?' "

Sande recalled that he looked at her, and then stared at the house.

"Very slowly, he turned back and stared directly at me," Sande said, "Then, he said, 'It's kind of late. . . . You'd better be careful.' "

The man looked again at the house. It appeared to Sande that he saw someone looking out the window at the two of them.

"He must have thought that I wasn't alone, that someone inside was watching and waiting for me to come in," Sande said. "I was so shook that when I got inside my legs gave way. I was shaking. It was an overreaction to the encounter outside."

Sande said she had heard lots of tales over the years about the Parson Thorne Mansion being haunted.

One suggested the downstairs kitchen is haunted. Another said the wife or daughter of one of the owners, or a builder, died while the mansion or additions were being constructed and she still haunts the home.

After about a year and a half, Sande moved to Dover, because it was a shorter commute to her job. Interestingly, her ghost had nothing to do with the departure.

"I never felt afraid in that house," she said, thinking back to at least two instances when the watchful specter of Parson Thorne Mansion played a direct role in protecting her from possible harm.

Parson Thorne Mansion

INN*formation*

Inncidentally: The Mansion is open to the public from 2-4 p.m. on the first Saturday and Sunday of each month, May through October, and at other times by appointment. Admission is $1 per person. Milford Historical Society members and children are admitted free. The property is listed on the National Register of Historic Places and is designated a Milford Landmark.

A framed document in the kitchen lists the owners of "Silver Hill," from the 17th century to the present. A gift shop in the east wing on the first level offers maps, area books and souvenirs for sale.

Innteresting note: Some people seem to attract spirits, or are at least comfortable living with them. This may be the case with Sande Warren Price, who currently is administrator of Woodburn, Delaware's Governor's Mansion in historic Dover. It's said at least four spirits haunt the official governor's residence, which was featured in *Opening the Door*, Volume II of the *Spirits Between the Bays Series*.

The Ghost is Inn: In the first floor kitchen, in the private areas of the second floor apartment and in the attic.

To get Inn touch: The Parson Thorne Mansion, 501 N.W. Front Street, Milford, DE 19963; telephone (302) 422-3115

Chapter illustration courtesy of the Parson Thorne Mansion/Milford Historical Society

Joseph of the Kemp House Inn

When Colonel Joseph Kemp started building his three-story, Federal-era, brick home in 1807, St. Michaels, Maryland, was nothing like the busy, Eastern Shore tourist mecca that exists today.

In the mid 1600s, when the area was first settled, the town's location on the Upper Chesapeake at the water's edge made it a perfect site for ship building, fishing and associated maritime trades.

Some believe the Episcopal church, made of logs in 1677, was named after Saint Michael the Archangel, and the town's name came from being associated with that structure. In the 18th century, when tobacco was a major Maryland crop, St. Michaels was an ideal site for overseas shipping, and the town was the residence to many sailors, craftsmen, merchants, sea captains and professional people.

During the War of 1812, when the population of St. Michaels was about 300 persons living in approximately 50 homes, the British sailed into the harbor and attacked the town. The invaders were interested in St. Michaels because it was known as a center of privateers, blockade runners and shipyards. According to historians, the local militia—the St. Michaels Patriotic Blues under the command of Colonel Joseph Kemp—contributed to the defense of the town during the August 1813 invasion.

The most successful technique employed by the American defenders was the decision to tie lanterns to branches in the highest treetops and at the tips of the masts of vessels moored in the St. Michaels harbor. With all the town lights extinguished, this effective use of a diversionary technique caused British gunners to overshoot the residential areas and there were no casualties. The only house hit is now known as the Cannonball House, located on Mulberry Street.*

✳   ✳   ✳   ✳

Situated on the very edge of the business district on centrally located Talbot Street, the Kemp House Inn is, literally, within footsteps of St. Michaels shops, pubs and museums.

The building opened originally under the name Smithton Inn in April 1982, and current, on-site manager Pat Evans has been working at the establishment since September of that year. She has catered to thousands of tourists and responded to the needs of three different owners.

Pat said the white brick building on the corner of Talbot and West Chestnut Streets had been vacant for a short time, and also served for a few years as a funeral parlor before becoming an inn. She said the name was eventually changed to honor the home's builder and original resident.

There are seven rooms in the main house, five with private bath and the two third-floor rooms share bathroom facilities. Interestingly, there are no public rooms, such as a dining room, parlor or recreation area. Therefore, Pat said, breakfast is served to guests in their rooms, except in the months of pleasant weather when many visitors decide to eat on the attractive brick patio.

Located on the side of the inn, the patio area is surrounded by a white, wooden fence and full-grown boxwoods. There also is a cottage, with private bath, located to the rear of the main building near the patio, that is available for rent.

Seated in the Brown Room, just to the right of the first-floor entrance hallway, inn manager Pat stressed that she, personally, is a non-believer. However, she was willing to share a few stories

---

*A detailed version of the events surrounding the British land and sea attacks on St. Michaels in August 1813 can be found in the book *St. Michaels: The Town That Fooled the British*, by Gilbert Byron and illustrated by John Moll, published by St. Mary's Square Museum, Inc., St. Michaels, Md. It is available in many local shops.

that she had heard over the years, from other workers and guests, about the building's friendly spiritual resident.

"There was a young girl who worked here," Pat said, "and she was in the hall, at the bottom of the stairway, when she said she saw a blue streak flash by and head up the stairs.

"She couldn't describe it any better than that. Then, she said, 'It must be Joseph, heading up the steps.' "

Pat explained that the ghost is often referred to as "Joseph," because that was the name of the original owner, Colonel Joseph Kemp, and the name just sort of caught on.

"The girl was never afraid of him. In fact, she said he was just a friendly little guy," recalled Pat, who pointed out that nearly all of the unusual activity seems to occur in the Blue Room, located on the second floor directly above the street-level Gold Room.

"I've never seen or felt anything during all these years" said Pat. Then, pausing a moment, she added, "Well, I will say that sometimes, when it's quiet and when I have occasion to go into the Blue Room . . . . there's just something different.

"In the daytime, it's quiet, relaxing. But, in the evenings, it makes me a little uneasy. There's a different kind of feeling."

Apparently, Pat is not the only one who senses something odd. When her daughter-in-law, Diana, was helping out at the inn recently, the younger woman said she heard a door slam when she was sure there was no one else in the building.

Pat recalled that the worker, who had seen the blue streak in the mid 1980s, complained that towels she had folded and stacked on shelves in the laundry area were tossed down on top of the washer and dryer.

" 'Oh, Joseph's been down here messing around,' she would say," Pat remembered.

During the Christmas holidays, two women were staying in the Blue Room. They both had brought gifts to share with each other. After they made the exchange, they went out to dinner. When they came back, the wrappings and ribbons, which they had placed in the trash can in the Blue Room, were scattered all over the floor.

"Maybe," said Pat, laughing at the thought, "we have a playful, little Christmas ghost here with us, too."

Pausing for a moment, Pat then added, "The interesting thing is that all of these incidents, that I wrote down to tell you, have occurred in the same room. And they were experienced by people who never had any contact with each other, and who knew nothing about the other events which took place in the room. And they all happened a year or two apart. It wasn't like something happened every week."

Pat said a middle-aged couple was staying over in the Blue Room. During the night, the woman had a strange feeling that someone was in the room beside her. She sat up in bed, and her husband was asleep beside her. She saw the rocking chair moving slowly back and forth a few times. Then, it stopped.

"She told me she felt a little uneasy," Pat recalled. "Then she went back to sleep. She told me the whole story the next morning."

The last event involved a father and son in the Blue Room. The older man was in the four-poster bed, and the man in his 20s was sleeping in the trundle bed that pulled out from beneath the queen-sized mattress.

"The father said he awoke in the middle of the night," Pat said. "He thought someone was getting in bed with him. He could feel the pressure causing the queen mattress to sink, and he thought his son had gone to the bathroom and came back and forgot to get into the lower bed. But then the gentleman looked over and saw his son sleeping in the trundle bed, and it still felt like someone was in bed with him."

When asked how she reacts to these stories, Pat said she just listens and smiles.

Does she ever tell anyone about Joseph?

"No!" she said. "I don't think about Joseph if I can help it," the innkeeper said. "The young girl who worked here, the one who saw the blue streak, she made light of all of this. She enjoyed believing that these things happened, but not me."

Kemp House Inn
INN*formation*

Inncidentally: Robert E. Lee, a guest of Colonel Joseph Kemp, is believed to have stayed in the Yellow Room, located on the second floor across from the Blue Room. Several of the inn's rooms have operating fireplaces. Take notice of the polished brick floor on the first level of the inn, throughout the hallway and into the Brown and Gold Rooms. All of the rooms are furnished with period reproductions.

Innteresting notes: Restaurants, antique shops, gift stores and historical sites are plentiful in the town. Be sure to pick up a *Walking Tour of Saint Michaels* brochure, available free at most stores and inns.

The Ghost is Inn: The Blue Room on the second floor, the first-floor hallway and stairs leading up to the second level.

To get Inn touch: Kemp House Inn, 412 Talbot Street, Box 638, Saint Michaels, MD 21663; telephone (410) 745-2243.

Chapter illustration courtesy of The Kemp House Inn

The Inn At Mitchell House
and a Barrel of Rum

In the 1980s, Tracy Stone was working in the White House, reviewing correspondence addressed to President Ronald Reagan. Her husband, Jim, was teaching environmental and outdoor education at Sidwell Friends School in Washington, D.C.

Today, the young couple are innkeepers near Tolchester, in Kent County on Maryland's Eastern Shore. With help from their two children—Zach and Tory—and family cat, Mr. Magoo, they own and operate The Inn At Mitchell House.

The historic 18th-century manor house is surrounded by woods and situated on a knoll overlooking 10 rolling acres and picturesque Stoneybrook Pond.

But things were not always peaceful at the historic homestead. According to documents recorded in the Maryland Registry of old homesites, during the War of 1812 troops from the British Warship H.M.S. *Menelaus*, under the command of 28-year-old Sir Peter Parker, came ashore and marched through Kent County.

A slave alerted the local militia and, under the command of Lt. Col. Philip A. Reed, the Americans marched from Belle Air, now known as Fairlee, and encountered the British forces at the Battle of Caulk's Field.

On Aug. 31, 1814, the British sustained 15 casualties and they were forced to retreat. Carrying their seriously wounded leader, Sir Peter Parker, they headed back to their ship, which was anchored in the upper Chesapeake Bay. En route, they stopped at the Mitchell House to give the young naval officer emergency medical attention. Unfortunately, he lost a tremendous amount of blood and died in the Mitchell House kitchen.

Afterwards, his body was taken back to the ship. So that the officer's body could be preserved during the return voyage to England, the recently departed was placed in a barrel of rum.

It is not known if any of the *Menelaus* sailors availed themselves of the naval officer spirit's spirits during the long sea voyage back to the British Isles. But, upon its return, the body was buried in St. Margaret's, adjacent to Westminster Abbey.

After the Stones took over the inn, Tracy's father, Edward O'Donnell, figured that the British government must have a portrait of Sir Peter Parker. He contacted several British museums and, eventually, was able to secure a copy of a painting of the naval officer whose last breath was spent in Mitchell House. Today, a framed, color representation of Sir Peter Parker (1785-1814) hangs prominently in the center of the inn's Parlor Number One, off the main entrance hall.

Tracy considers the story an interesting historical anecdote. She mentioned that Kent County youngsters are taught the area legend in elementary school.

Providing more background on the stately building, Tracy and Jim said the original part of the dwelling was built about 1743. The three-story, brick addition was constructed by Joseph T. Mitchell in 1825. That landowner at one time commanded an estate of approximately 1,200 acres, with long stretches of shoreline on the nearby Chesapeake Bay.

Today, the home features six guest rooms, five with private bath, all named after local historical persons or sites. These. include the Joseph T. Mitchell Room, Martha Hynson Room, Dr. William Ringgold Room, Col. Philip Reed Room, Black Hall Hermitage and Sir Peter Parker Room.

"He never stayed here," said Tracy, "but he died in the kitchen which is just below his room, so it seemed fitting to name the bedroom after him."

With all this history and character, one can't help but wonder if any ghosts reside within the inn's 250-year-old walls.

Tracy and Jim offer knowing smiles. . . pause . . . and then begin to share their more unusual, unexplained experiences. All, or at least most, they stress, have been of a friendly nature.

The house has been an inn only since 1982, said Jim. In 1986, he and Tracy purchased the property, along with many of its furnishings, from the inn's former owners.

A little more than a year after they had moved in, the couple visited the inn's former owners. After dinner, the previous innkeepers shared some of the strange things that had happened when they owned The Inn At Mitchell House.

They said the Col. Philip Reed Room, also referred to as Bedroom Number 4 located in the original farmhouse section, contained a rocking chair. That rocker, they said, sometimes moved back and forth by itself, without anyone in it.

As the evening progressed, the new owners discovered that the former owners' basset hound would enjoy spending time inside that room, and it would act as if it were playing with some unknown person or, perhaps, another dog.

Tracy said that Mr. Magoo, her family's cat, is king of the inn and can be found sauntering through every room. But, it will not go into Bedroom Number 4. It's as if it is afraid of what is inside.

"There have been guests who have sat in the rocking chair," said Jim, "and they claim they felt something brush against their legs, as if it were a dog ghost passing by."

One guest, Jim recalled, came out of the room one morning and said to the innkeeper, "There's something in that room, isn't there?" But he said it very calmly, even matter-of-factly, not upset, Jim added.

Tracy admitted that she has never seen the chair rocking, but she has removed it from the room and placed it in the basement.

Why?

"It was looking a bit ragged and beat up," she said. Then, slowly raising her eyes as if embarrassed, she added, "I guess I could have fixed it, but then . . . ."

About three weeks after the couple moved into the property, they hosted a retreat of seven priests. Being Catholic, Tracy asked them to bless the house, for no other reason than it was a longstanding family custom.

Jim said it was very impressive to see seven priests in the main hallway, praying for the inn and its new residents.

"To be honest," Tracy said, "we had just moved in. I was home a lot by myself. It's an old house, and I heard funny noises and was a bit scared."

Since they have owned the property, Tracy said there were two female psychics who stayed at the inn, each on a different occasion.

"They both told me they had the ability to experience spirits," said Tracy. "They asked if it would be okay, and I gave them permission to check the place out. I even let them into the attic and basement."

In both instances, that occurred more than a year apart, the women told Tracy that it was a friendly, warm home. Even the Philip Reed Room offered a comfortable aura. However, an area in the corner of the basement presented a different sensation.

"There's a corner in the furnace room," Tracy said, "that's creepy."

She added that one psychic said there is sometimes an area where certain things are pushed toward a corner. The other psychic told the couple that "the basement held something bad."

Laughing, Tracy said, "That's where my laundry room is. So it gives me an excuse not to go down there."

Jim said that until 30 years ago there were shackles, that had been used to chain slaves, still hanging in the basement, but they were removed and the areas had been patched over.

One architectural historian told the couple that it was highly unusual to find shackles located under a plantation owner's living space. But Tracy wondered why that would be the case, especially since the slaves were considered to be highly valuable.

Sitting in Parlor Number Two, Jim and Tracy discussed the significance of their home and its character and historical value.

"If the walls could talk," she said, "imagine what secrets they could share. There have been so many deaths and births in this house. And it's amazing that it has such a light, friendly atmosphere.

"I absolutely enjoy it. If I was remotely uncomfortable, I would have been out of here a long time ago. I've never been scared so much that it has bothered me."

"But," Jim added, "there have been a few nights that she has hit me on the side in the middle of the night and sent me downstairs to check on noises and things."

"I find it all very interesting," said Tracy. "If there is something here, whatever it is, it is nice. And it can stay here."

The Inn At Mitchell House
INN*formation*

Inncidentally: There are six guest rooms, five with private bath. The inn can accommodate small business meetings and weddings. Attractive Stoneybrook Pond is on the property near the inn. Guests have the use of a private beach and tennis courts a half-mile from the inn. Be sure to meet Ed the Elk and Isaac the Moose, both located in the inn's kitchen.

Innteresting notes: The Inn At Mitchell House offers evening dining for the public on Fridays and Sundays in its authentic 18th-century dining room. Reservations are required 24 hours in advance. Tracy does the cooking and Jim cleans the dishes.

The Ghost is Inn: Bedroom Number 4, the Colonel Philip Reed Room. Sir Peter Parker died from battle wounds in the first-floor kitchen.

To get Inn touch: The Inn At Mitchell House, 8796 Maryland Parkway, Chestertown, MD 21620; telephone (410) 778-6500.

Chapter illustration courtesy of The Inn At Mitchell House

Spirited Guests in the Blue Coat Inn

Some visitors to the Blue Coat Inn in Dover, Delaware, are reluctant to return their menus, for they offer fascinating historical information on the area surrounding Delaware's capital city.

According to the Inn's menu, the region of the St. Jones River is one of the most historic in the First State. Paleo-era Indians lived and traded on its banks more than 10,000 years ago. In the 17th century, it was first charted by Swedish explorers who called the area "Wolf Creek." Later the lands were settled by English and Welsh contemporaries of William Penn, and, eventually, landowners and farmers developed large tracts, producing lumber, grain and tobacco, that was shipped in vessels built on the creek banks.

Delaware heroes and patriots—including Caesar Rodney, John Dickinson and Vincent Loockerman—walked the paths and main roads of the area that are still traveled today.

In the 1960s, John Koutoufaris and Roger Keith, two brothers-in-law, bought a spacious private residence, with four stone fireplaces, that had been built on the banks of Silver Lake in 1948.

During remodeling, weathered timbers from local barns were installed under the direction of George Bennett, formerly of Colonial Williamsburg and author of *Early Architecture of Delaware*.

When the Blue Coat Inn opened in 1967, its atmosphere gave patrons the impression that the restaurant had been an historic traveling stop for more than a century.

Current owners Marlene and John Koutoufaris are proud of their establishment, which has catered to both locals and tourists for more than 25 years.

The inn's name refers to the "blue coat" worn by Colonel John Haslett's Colonial Delaware Regiment. Haslett led the soldiers from the Dover Green in August 1776 to join General Washington's army and the unit fought in almost every major encounter in the Revolutionary War.

Unlike most state units, whose members wore whatever civilian style clothing they owned, the Delaware contingent was considered among the best uniformed and equipped. According to Christopher Ward in *The Delaware Continentals*, in addition to the distinctive blue coats, Delawareans wore black-jacked leather hats with a high front peak, inscribed with the Delaware Crest, including a full-rigged ship and a sheaf of wheat. During parades and formal ceremonies the officers and men added red feathered plumes to the left side of their caps. From the color of the coats they were known as the "Delaware Blues."

Walking through the Blue Coat Inn, one is aware of the attention to historic detail in the rooms, each of which has a specific theme associated with some aspect of Delaware history.

•Three Counties Room features a portrait of William Penn and a coat of arms of Lord de la Warr;

•Independence Room honors Caesar Rodney, Thomas McKean and George Read, all patriots of the Revolution;

•Liberty Room proclaims the state motto "Liberty and Independence" and features a portrait of John Dickinson, land owner, patriot and Delaware and Pennsylvania governor;

•George Tavern is named for two famous Georges—President George Washington and King George III;

•Commodore Rooms recognize Delaware naval heroes of the War of 1812—Jacob Jones and Thomas Macdonough; and

•Sailing Eagle Tavern honors vessels of the Delaware River and Bay and features a portrait of Capt. William Kidd, the infamous pirate who raided and terrorized the Delaware Coast.

✻　　✻　　✻　　✻

But as one looks past the inn's appearance and begins to focus on the unusual events that have occurred in the buildings, the question "Why" comes to mind.

Perhaps it was the old barn planking.

Maybe it was the attention to detail that has created an ambiance that encourages patrons to imagine what it was like in 18th-century Dover.

Could it be the sensitivity of the owners to spirit vibrations?

Possibly, it's the historic artifacts and paintings that have been so carefully selected.

Who will ever know the reason why?

Best, instead, to share the stories.

While neither of them can offer a logical explanation, both Marlene and John believe the Blue Coat Inn is the site of "spirit visitations." Those are the words that Marlene uses when she refers to inexplicable events that have also been witnessed by long- and short-term employees at the inn.

Sitting at a corner table on a cold winter afternoon, the couple shared the first incident that occurred soon after they opened the restaurant. John said he recalled going up into the attic, which is quite long and is very dark, even during the day. The attic runs the length of the building, and he said a force of some kind seemed to be "encouraging" him to walk deeper into the darkness.

He followed the invisible beckoning to a location that was about halfway to the end of the building—and a considerable distance from the doorway and light switch. Suddenly, realizing where he was but not knowing why he went there, he turned and was alarmed by some sense of a presence he could not explain. Yelling, he ran toward the open door and the safety of the hallway.

Months later, John walked into the building after closing one night. Everything, he said, had been turned off when he left hours before. After wandering around the inn for at least five minutes, he entered the kitchen and noticed that the radio was playing.

But no one was there, there was no reason for it to be on.

It wasn't long after that, said Marlene, that a fellow who worked for them at night, as both a custodian and watchman, said he heard footsteps, doors opening and closing and toilets flushing by themselves.

"He suggested we call a plumber to see what was wrong with the toilets," recalled Marlene. "Eventually, he brought one of his children to work with him, and the child would stay and watch TV during the night. He didn't want to be here alone.

"We eventually realized that while our spirits will play tricks on us, they're not the kind we need to be afraid of. Everything they have done has been funny or for a reason."

John agreed, sharing one of many helpful incidents.

The owner went into the lounge to adjust the thermostat for the night. It was dark, and he could not see the reading. Not wanting to bother to walk over to the light switch, he thought to himself, *Ghost, I wish I had something that would help me see.*

Looking down, he saw a book of matches . . . but, he added, most definitely, that the matches had not been there seconds before.

"On another evening, about midnight," said John, "I had locked up and was leaving the restaurant through the rear gate. Suddenly, I heard a clicking, or tapping, on glass, as if someone were tapping on the window from inside, trying to get my attention. I heard it three times.

"It was like, click, click click," he said, flicking his fingers against the top of a water glass.

"I turned and noticed that I had left the window open, the only window where the sound could have come from."

"The spirit was telling him not to leave," said Marlene, "and was alerting him to go back and shut the window. It was very helpful."

John admitted that the ghost can be a bit unsettling, but he has learned to deal with it.

"When I'm here by myself," he said, "even in the daytime, I feel like someone is with me. Sometimes, it makes the hair on my arm stand on end. A few Mondays ago, when we were closed, I was fixing some tile. I suddenly felt someone looking over me. At those times, I turn and say, 'Be a good boy. Don't scare me.' And things calm down right away." Then, pausing to offer a wide smile, John added, "I think the ghost likes me."

While John and Marlene seem to be understanding spirit hosts, their tolerant attitude may not be shared by all their employees. Some workers have had experiences they would rather forget. Others have done a disappearing act to rival the building's phantoms and moved on.

After closing, late one night, a bus boy was walking through the Sailing Eagle Tavern. Most of the lights were off and it was dark. Carrying a tray of glasses, he was taking slow, careful steps.

32

Glancing ahead, he noticed a kind looking man about 65 years of age, leaning against the bulkhead divider. At first, the boy smiled. The man nodded back. Then, with his eyes at the floor for only a second, the boy realized the building was closed and only workers should be inside.

Quickly raising his eyes, he discovered the man was gone.

The boy went immediately into the kitchen to tell John and the maitre d'.

"I guess you know it was the ghost," John told the boy.

"I don't believe in that stuff!" the young man replied.

When he finished his work, the boy left the building, heading for his car. Suddenly, he came running back inside the restaurant, shouting for anyone to come to him.

The boy, visibly shaken, told John that he saw the same man, from the bar, again. He was staring at the boy from behind a window in the Stable Shoppes, the inn's nearby gift store.

"I said to him, 'I thought you didn't believe this stuff.' And he said, 'I'm not going by the gift shop alone!' So we walked him to his car, and a couple of days later he quit," John said.

In the same room, Mary Priester, a 27-year employee, was tending bar when a champagne glass, that had been resting on a shelf, came crashing to the floor.

"If I had been here all by myself," Mary recalled, "I'd have thought I'd gone crazy. The customers looked at me, and I looked at them, then I said, 'I guess it's just the ghost again.' "

On a different night, something or someone played three notes on the organ. It was unusual, said John, because there was no one else in the room, and the organ was turned off, unplugged and covered with a heavy canvass that ran from the top of the lid to the bottom at the floor.

"The bartender at that time was a short woman," recalled Marlene. "She ran around the bar and headed into the kitchen. She said if she had been taller she would have come across the bar."

In the reception area, near the cash register, John said one maitre d' saw a man standing near the cigarette machine, then turned and the image was gone.

"His description matched the older, friendly man who had been in the bar area several months earlier," said John. "At first the employee thought the man was waiting for someone to pick him up. But whoever it was vanished and the front door never opened or closed."

Marlene said the number of incidents causes memories to merge together, and it's impossible to keep track of exactly when they occurred. She remembered when one employee, from the Blue Coat Pancake House, came in with her husband for Thanksgiving dinner.

The couple was seated in the dining area in the Sailing Eagle Tavern. It was midday, about 1 p.m., when the woman asked her husband why the little boy in the white shirt was staring at them.

When her husband turned to look, he did not see the boy, who, his wife said, was about 9 years old.

During the latter part of the meal, when the wife came back from the ladies room, she whispered to her husband, "Look. There he is again. The boy is back!"

As her husband turned and saw no one, he asked his wife if she was feeling well. The boy, whom she claimed had approached within her reach at table side, had disappeared again.

Debbie Cooper, a 25-year kitchen employee, said, "I've seen a lot of strange things happen." She casually mentioned pie plates and other items flying off shelves, containers moving and ice coolers sliding across counters.

"When they happen, we just look at each other and laugh. What else can you do?" asked Debbie, with a shrug. "We say, 'Oh! It's the ghost again.'

"The new people never believe any of it in the beginning. But when something happens, they have second thoughts about what we told them. Then they get strange looks on their faces."

During a heavy snow one winter, said Marlene, three employees stayed overnight in the front reception room.

"But," said John, laughing, "they were too scared to sleep, because they were listening for the ghost."

Word of the Blue Coat's spirits has spread beyond the First State. The *National Enquirer* weekly tabloid ran a feature on June 22, 1993, about the Ghost Chasers Society, a Delaware-based group of spirit hunters. A photograph accompanying the article was taken in the Blue Coat Inn, where the ghost hunters spent the night with sophisticated energy-detecting equipment. While they were not able to capture any evidence on tape, they did record high levels of energy.

Marlene said her son, Marc, received a call from a representative of a national television network following the article, but no camera crew ever arrived.

One psychic, who visited the inn, told the owners that the older ghost's name was John, and he is very happy about the inn and its display of Delaware history.

With the mention of that name, Marlene offered an interesting theory.

"John," she suggested, "may be Colonel John Haslett, leader of the Delaware militia. It is believed the large Irishman, who had left his medical practice to lead Delaware's troops against the British, died thinking he had never received just credit for what he considered was an outstanding career.

"We think he is thrilled because we dedicated the building in honor of his regiment, the Blue Coats," said Marlene. "We think he may feel safe here, and that he believes he's finally getting the recognition that he didn't get during his lifetime.

"Also, it's possible that the child may be a drummer boy, who was killed in one of the battles, and who may have been a favorite of Colonel Haslett."

When asked what they think of the ghostly attention their establishment has received, the owners give immediate answers in a manner that is both confident and comfortable.

"We don't hide the presence of the spirits," said Marlene. "Most people are skeptical, and others who believe are comfortable with the idea. I never feel like I'm completely alone. I feel safe here all the time."

John admitted that he doesn't visit the inn alone at night.

"But I will come in during the day," said John. "I turn on the lights and pause at each doorway as I go from room to room. I often say, 'Hi! I'm here!' "

"Sometimes," added Marlene, "things will be moved, like flower arrangements on the tables, a desk chair, or we will find other little things out of place. I think they're trying, in little subtle ways, to remind us that they are here. I will admit that I love their being here, and I don't want them to leave."

The Blue Coat Inn
INN*formation*

Inncidentally: The Blue Coat Inn's decor is an organized display of Delaware history from its settlement through the period of the War of 1812. During restoration of the Delaware State House to match its 1791 appearance, the 1910 tower was removed. Its midsection was salvaged and stands as the inn's Lakeside Pavilion, complete with the decorative Blue Hen spire and a diamond-shaped boxwood garden.

The restaurant is closed on Mondays. Lunch and dinner are served daily. The gift shop operates during about the same hours as the restaurant.

Innteresting notes: The adjacent Stable Shoppes features collectibles and Delaware memorabilia. According to Marlene Koutoufaris, that building was originally used as a stable for thoroughbreds of the home's original owners Mr. and Mrs. George Lacy Griffith of Dover.

The inn parking lot was once a pasture, and Mrs. Griffith's favorite English thoroughbred was buried under a large tree in the center. The present owners were not to disturb the remains of the horse, and the area surrounding the tree was paved. Over the years, the tree was struck several times by lightning. For safety, the tree was removed but the remains of the horse were not disturbed. A circle in the paving is visible where the tree once stood.

The Ghost is Inn: Events have occurred in the attic, upstairs office, kitchen, reception area, in both the bar and dining areas of the Sailing Eagle Tavern and in the Stable Shoppes.

To get Inn touch: The Blue Coat Inn, on Silver Lake, 800 North State Street, Dover, DE 19901; telephone (302) 674-1776.

Chapter illustration courtesy of The Blue Coat Inn

FORT DELAWARE.

Resurrecting More than the Past at Fort Delaware

When there's not too much tourist activity, particularly in the winter months, stand on the dock in Delaware City and look east, out toward Pea Patch Island. The stillness of the passing water and the clear open sky frame a portrait in time of the Civil War-era citadel known as Fort Delaware.

Gaze at the distant gray and red structure of brick and granite in the early morning—when the mist and fog hover over the surface of the river, fighting to survive a few more precious moments before the sun burns them off—and you travel into another dimension . . . where the past still exists.

That view, now in the closing days of the 20th century, is exactly the same scene as was experienced by Union and Confederate troops when they boarded wooden boats and headed for the island during the Civil War, more than 130 years ago.

✳ ✳ ✳ ✳

Mention Fort Delaware and legends, stories and folklore abound. One of the better known peninsula tales refers to the controversy over how the island got its name and when it actually came into existence.

According to the late Delaware journalist, W. Emerson Wilson—in his short book entitled, *Fort Delaware*, published by the

University of Delaware Press—Colonial maps did not even indicate that the island existed at that bend in the Delaware River.

An often repeated story is that a boat loaded with beans or peas was grounded on a shoal in that area of the Delaware River. After its cargo was spilled, the peas eventually sprouted, took root and the island grew to its present size.

Major Pierre L'Enfant, who designed the layout of Washington, D.C., recommended in the late 1700s that a fort be built on the island. During the War of 1812, the first fortifications were erected. Various battlements and structures were present during the next 40 years. But, according to Wilson, it was not until 1859 that the present fort was complete, and "constructed in the shape of a pentagon, with granite outside walls and brick casemates within."

The rationale, that existed from the Civil War and through the days of World War II, is that Fort Delaware's location on the island—plus the accompanying defenses at Fort Mott on the New Jersey coast and Fort du Pont on the Delaware shore—would protect the major port of Philadelphia from enemy attack.

But Fort Delaware and its defenders were to see none of the heroic action that provides material for glorious paintings featuring brave soldiers in battle scenes.

No enemy flags were captured on its surrounding grounds, no major battles were won or lost, no cavalry charges were signaled by the bugle's call. Instead, the impressive garrison, with its dark, thick walls and 30-foot-wide moat—complete with drawbridge—gained its infamous reputation as nothing more than a common, depressing prison camp.

In April 1862, 258 Confederate soldiers, many from Virginia, arrived on Pea Patch Island. Since there were never any plans that the fortress accommodate captives, the Confederates were housed in small windowless rooms that had originally been built to hold ammunition.

The damp compartments were ventilated with only small slits in the brickwork, and little air was able to enter or leave the enclosed areas. The sites eventually were referred to as "dungeons." According to Wilson's research, old newspaper articles about the fort written after the war stated that these rooms had contained wooden planks—long since removed—that were inscribed with initials and messages from the prisoners, dating back to April 1862.

As the war progressed, more Confederates were sent to Fort Delaware. Eventually, the numbers grew to more than 12,500. The highest number was reached in July 1863, immediately following the Battle of Gettysburg.

To accommodate the large numbers, wooden barracks were built outside the fort and these buildings covered a major portion of the island. Disease, however, took a heavy toll on the prison population and hundreds of Confederates left the island in pine boxes to be buried at Fort Mott in New Jersey.

Civil War experts often refer to the deplorable conditions at the Confederate operated prison in Andersonville, Georgia. However, according to statistics, the death rate at Fort Delaware was higher than Andersonville's. As a result, the Pea Patch Island fortress earned the infamous title: "Andersonville of the North." Most of the deaths, records show, were from poor living conditions and rampant disease.

Newspaper accounts indicate there were numerous prison transfers as well as several escapes from the island.

Some Confederate escapees were returned to the dungeons, others were never caught and some, no doubt, were unable to reach the Delaware or New Jersey shorelines and perished in the depths of the Delaware River.

Do these drowned ghosts, along with the spirits of those who died on the island, still search for their Southern homeland?

Who is to know?

But those who work at Fort Delaware, plus visitors to the island, tell their own strange tales . . . some worth considering, others certainly worth telling.

These stories give the impression that some restless spirits of the more than 33,000 Southern prisoners and thousands of Union troops who lived on Pea Patch may still roam the gray stone fort, stand guard at its ancient drawbridge and inhabit the secluded island's silent, marshy hallowed ground.

Lee Jennings is a straightforward type of guy. Present him a question and you get a direct, immediate answer. Ask him if there are ghosts at Fort Delaware and he's not at all surprised. In fact, he delivers a broad smile, as if he's well prepared for the inquiry.

"One of the top 10 questions we get about Fort Delaware is: 'Where are the ghosts?' "

An historical interpreter who has greeted thousands of visitors each year in the persona of former Fort Delaware Battery Commander Capt. Stanislaus Mlotkowski, Lee has done extensive research about both the fort and the lives of its former Yankee and Rebel occupants.

"Fort Delaware tells a story all by itself," he said, during a conversation one winter evening in his home. Although he lives several miles away from the fort, it is never far from his thoughts. It's also apparent that he enjoys the opportunity to discuss the site and its important role in history.

"I don't encourage ghosts," Lee said, "but it's important for Delaware and the country to know the story of the fort and its role in our country's history."

Press him further, however, and he begins to share bits and pieces, mainly hearsay about spectral experiences.

There's the story, he said, that has been passed around for years of the people who took a photograph near a cannon. When it was developed, they claimed to see a Civil War soldier standing next to the living person who was the subject of the picture.

Nearly everyone's heard about the footsteps, voices, moans and cries coming from the dungeons. These areas were originally powder magazines, but they were later used as solitary confinement for unruly prisoners.

Two students on a class tour said they saw a pale white glow in one of the powder magazines, located to the right of the drawbridge entrance.

"We saw it and kept going," one of the boys said. "It wasn't bright at all. It was more like a blob. It sounded like creaking bones. We kept going and didn't turn around, and we didn't go back to take another look, either."

Then there is the talk of hauntings in the casemates, the hallways behind the fortress walls that were built with openings and slits for the defenders' guns.

Lee said he has heard all types of stories.

"Go walk in the casemates or sit in the general's office for a while," Lee said, "and you hear the voices. You can't be here and listen and not hear or feel something. We have all felt something, when you go through those long, dark hallways that run on the south side of the fort. You walk along and you hear footsteps behind you. In the beginning, you think there's one person following you, and by the time you're halfway through it sounds like there are 30 or 40 walking back there.

"It's wet, dripping. There are varmints scurrying in the corners, and bats and pigeons flying out. Even if you're not superstitious, it will still scare you."

In the mid 1940s, the federal government abandoned Fort Delaware. In the following years, vandals stripped the structure of nearly everything that was not nailed down.

Today, extensive security precautions are in place. Guarding the fort at night are two large German Shepherds. Spook, who is all white, and the brown-colored Dingle are let loose to roam the fort's interior grounds when the staff locks up and leaves.

"They are considered the last prisoners of Fort Delaware," explained Lee, with a laugh. "Spook is serving a life sentence for killing a chicken."

He stressed that the staff is the last to leave and the first to arrive at the fort. They lock the doors and they open them up the next day.

One summer morning, after arriving and caring for the dogs, Lee and two colleagues began to inspect the grounds and rooms. On one wall of the Polish Society Museum Room, operated by the Capt. Stanislaus Mlotkowski Memorial Brigade Society, there is a large portrait of Capt. Leon Jastremski, a Southern officer of Polish descent who was a prisoner at the fort. On this day, the painting was resting on the floor, leaning against the wall directly below where it normally hangs.

"It's a huge picture, weighing at least 60 lbs, with the frame," said Lee. "It hangs on the wall five feet above the ground. If it had fallen off, it would have shattered into a thousand pieces. It sits on a one-inch long nail, that was perfectly fine. There's no way this should have happened. We thought this was pretty strange."

Stranger yet was the coincidence of the date the undamaged painting was moved and discovered.

Lee explained that Jastremski was captured three times during the Civil War and was sent to Fort Delaware twice. He also was a member of "The Immortal Six Hundred," a group of Confederate officers who were involved in a prisoner exchange in 1864. That transfer eventually resulted in the Rebs being forced, by their Union captors, to stand under fire by their own Confederate guns at Morris Island in Charlestown Harbor.

The date that Jastremski's painting was found resting on the floor was the anniversary of the day when he left Fort Delaware for Morris Island.

"There was no rational explanation for what happened," Lee said. "No one else goes in and out of the rooms. You cannot get in there after we leave. Sometime during the night, it just fell, or sat, down."

While Lee said he has never seen a ghost at the fort, his wife admitted that she has.

Casually, Linda Jennings mentioned that when she was young, walking through cemeteries and reading tombstones was as normal as a day at the mall, so experiences with the supernatural do not bother her.

Linda explained that part of her involvement at Fort Delaware is presenting living history in the kitchen area. On these occassions, she and several other women and their children dress in Civil War-era clothing and prepare food in the manner of the period.

It was in the back kitchen, behind the officers' quarters, where she saw the ghost.

"I looked over in the corner," Linda said, "and I saw a lady staring at us. I did a double take and kind of nodded. Because there were children with me, I didn't say anything."

Linda described the lady as a black woman, about 35 years old and 5'6" tall. She had a scar on her left cheek and wore a blue-and-white, checkered dress with a white collar.

"Her apron was filthy, cruddy," Linda said. "It was singed at the bottom, probably from working in the kitchen. She was there for about an hour. She walked around, came close and examined what we were cooking. She was looking in the pots. She vanished for a short time and then came back.

"She looked at me. I felt she was nodding approval at what we were doing."

Lee said there were quite a few free blacks who were employed as help in the kitchens and laundry, both in and outside the fort. Having a black cook would have been normal in the Union officers' quarters.

"I wanted to try to talk to her," Linda said. "But I didn't get the opportunity. The kids were here cutting carrots and potatoes and onions, and I didn't want to do anything in front of them."

Linda had the impression that at first the Civil War phantom was wondering what was taking place. Then, after the tours of visitors passed through, the ghost realized that the volunteers were reenacting the past, offering a presentation of what things were like during the Civil War at the fort.

 Is such a sighting possible?

"I'm an historian, " said Lee. "I know my wife is sensitive to these types of activities more than I am. I believe, and I attach importance to what she says. We have some payroll records of those who worked at the fort. I'd like to see what we can find."

Is it possible that the spirits are responding to the setting and portrayals of the past?

Could it be that accurate representations of the long passed era—with Civil War uniforms, food and equipment—cause resident ghosts to be more comfortable and encourage them to appear?

"I think they are here because we are here," said Linda. "They can be there all the time, and we just don't see them."

"Maybe the familiar surroundings help," replied Lee. "I recall when we started there, walking through the dungeon areas was unpleasant. It was not a nice place to be. You would start out walking, and you end up running to get out.

"But the further we got into the living history program, some of those feelings started to go away. A lot of the uneasiness seemed to disappear. Things seemed to calm down a lot. We had a feeling we had their approval, that we were telling the story and we were telling it right."

Fort Delaware
INN*formation*

INNcidentally: The state park, including Pea Patch Island and the fort, is under the jurisdiction of the Division of Parks and Recreation of the Delaware Department of Natural Resources and Environmental Control. Volunteer assistance is provided by members of the Fort Delaware Society, which has a wide-ranging dues structure.

The fort is located on the island in the Delaware River. Access is by boat. The dock is located in Delaware City, several miles south of New Castle.

Fort Delaware is open weekends and holidays from the last weekend in April through September, 11 a.m.-6 p.m. From mid-June through Labor Day, the fort also is open from 11 a.m.-4 p.m. Wednesdays, Thursdays and Fridays. Admission to the fort is free. There is a charge for the round-trip boat transportation to and from the island, at $4.50 for adults and $3 for children under 14. Group tours are available.

INNteresting notes: Caution is recommended at certain sections of Fort Delaware. Be aware of signs alerting visitors to keep away from restricted and possibly hazardous areas. No child under the age of 15 is allowed in the fort unless accompanied by an adult. Children's groups inside the fort must be under the direct supervision of adults.

A model, built by the members of the Fort Delaware Society, located in the Museum Room, shows how the island and fort appeared in 1864.

The Living History Program is presented daily.

The Ghost is INN: Take a stroll in the area called the "dungeons." Other sightings or incidents have occurred in the powder magazines or dungeons to the left of the drawbridge entrance, the kitchen of the officers' quarters, in the Polish Society Museum Room and in the corner office of the administration building, which was occupied by the fort's commanding officer.

To get INN touch: To make group arrangements or for information, call (302) 834-7941. Information also is available from the Fort Delaware Society, P.O. Box 553, Delaware City, DE 19706; telephone (302) 834-1630.

Chapter illustration courtesy of Fort Delaware Society

Margaret
of the Bohemia House

Visitors to the Bohemia House Bed and Breakfast and Conference Center, located on Town Point Road south of Chesapeake City, Maryland, are impressed by its distinctive Victorian Italiante architecture, the striking decor and fine furnishings, 26 acres of pasture and woodlands, antique carriages, plus a picturesque view of both the Bohemia and Elk Rivers.

Stay the evening, or longer, as many regular guests do, and you will learn much more from resident hosts Sally and Herbert "Dick" Worsley.

During a quick, guided tour of the mansion, that was built around 1850 by the descendants of area historical figure Kitty Knight, the innkeepers offered an informal menu of American history with a heavy mix of local flavor.

They talked about the old, closed-up tunnel from the Bohemia River. At one time, it led to a large waiting room in the cellar of the house. It was used by slaves who were escaping to the North during the mid 1800s as a stop on the Underground Railroad.

Lifting an Oriental rug, Dick pointed to the trap door in the main entrance hallway. He said it was used to store and hide grain from sudden inspections by passing Union troops during the Civil War.

Sally led the way into the basement. Heading into a far corner of the musty, 140-year-old, maze-like cellar, with flashlight in hand, she entered a room used by one of the workers.

45

To try to make sure nothing entered his bedroom, the man had pushed a heavy piece of furniture against the small doorway that led to the catacombs.

Sally pushed aside the wooden dresser and opened up a small crawl space door. Her flashlight's thin beam pierced the damp darkness and illuminated the crumbling stone archway that she said marks the edge of one of the uncharted, honeycombed paths.

"There are lots of tunnels down there," she said. "They're called the catacombs and some are closed off. We can't tell why they were dug or where they go."

No one is eager to crawl down and explore them, she added. especially, with all the snakes and wild varmints that over the years have claimed the dark lanes as their home.

But, she added, even more interesting is the story of the catacombs told by some local folks.

Many believe one of the home's former residents—Margaret, who was the daughter of a wealthy Philadelphia baking company owner—may be buried somewhere under the house.

She disappeared in the 1920s and is yet to be found. Some say she was murdered and is buried in the bowels of the earthen tunnels under Bohemia House.

One neighbor told the Worsleys that he went down into the catacombs years ago and poked around with his shovel. The man claims he came upon a large mound of earth that looked like a grave. But, he became very upset and left in a rush after he found a woman's shoe and some scattered pieces of jewelry.

No body was ever discovered.

"We've heard some funny noises since we've been here," said Sally. "They say Margaret loved to play the organ. She played all day and night. We've even heard organ music at times. When we get up and go to investigate, we also hear what sounds like voices, as if people are talking at a party. Then, the closer you get, it fades out."

"I'm not a believer in ghosts," said Dick. But he said the unexplained music reminds him of the type gypsies would play around a campfire.

The spirit of that restless soul, said Sally, could be the inn's resident ghost, who seems to spend her evenings in the Elk Room, directly above the main entrance hall in the front of the building.

Sally said the delicate spirit seems to be sending signals by moving a heavy clock from the right side of the room's dresser to the other, opening a closet door, disturbing the bed covers and tossing artificial flowers from the window sill onto the floor.

"I make that bed, and it's as if someone has slept in it," Sally said. "The shape of a body, as if somebody has laid on it, is there. And no matter how many times you close the closet door, it's always open.

"The dog doesn't like to go into the Elk Room," Sally added. "And sometimes, when I'm running the vacuum, I see footprints on the rug. But I know that no one has been in there."

The other guest rooms—the Lord Baltimore, St. Augustine, Sassafras, Canal and Jacuzzi Suite—haven't yet given the hosts any indications of phantom residents.

But, said Sally, there is that dark, old, wooden rocker that seems to start up and move all by itself on the third floor landing.

Then, she paused and added with a smile, it could be the wind, perhaps a draft, or the settling timbers, or . . . whatever.

"If Margaret is here," said Sally, "I think she's very happy that we are here taking care of things."

"Except," she added after a few seconds, "maybe Margaret doesn't like artificial flowers, and that's why she throws them onto the floor."

Bohemia House
INN*formation*

Inncidentally: Sally, an Oklahoma native, and Dick, a jockey and horse trainer born in England, are resident managers of the eight-bedroom, seven-bath inn and conference center that can accommodate 60 participants for meetings.

Innteresting notes: Dick still trains thoroughbreds on the property. When requested, he will take out the inn's white Queen Elizabeth style, red-seated carriage, offering guests a memorable tour of the countryside. A newly constructed patio, outdoor pool, a three-hole golf course and several bicycles are available for guests' use.

The Ghost is Inn: The Elk Room, also known as Margaret's Room, on the second floor facing the entrance driveway.

To get Inn touch: Bohemia House Bed and Breakfast and Conference Center, 1236 Town Point Road, Chesapeake City, MD 21915; telephone (410) 885-3024.

Chapter illustration courtesy of the Bohemia House

Home
of the
Penman of the Revolution

Talk to those who work in the John Dickinson Plantation every day—as administrators, guides and historical interpreters—and they are unanimous in their response that no ghosts, spirits or unusual beings have been spotted in the buildings or on the grounds.

However, according to local legends and town gossip, and an interesting reference in Dennis William Hauck's *The National Directory of Haunted Places*, John Dickinson—the well-known Colonial lawyer, who is called the "Penman of the Revolution" for his published essays on Colonial rights and liberty—may still be about.

Some claim Dickinson, or another restless family spirit, can be heard writing and scratching away with a quill pen in the small Book Room, located to the left of the plantation home's main entrance hall.

Others, who have visited the building, say that the ghost occasionally rests and naps in the bed in the large second-floor master bedroom, not bothering to smooth out the spreads and covers when it rises to roam.

There also are reports that certain police officers who sometimes must respond to the secluded site, located immediately south of the Dover, Delaware, Air Force Base, are not thrilled to respond alone, without a partner, to the plantation.

Oftentimes, alone and in the middle of the night, they must check out the buildings and grounds of the isolated 250-year-old

49

plantation. And, some claim, they have heard unexplained sounds and seen things that they would rather not discuss.

But all that shouldn't be surprising. After all, the area is isolated, and the structure is old, and there is that burial ground off to the side of the main house . . . and, especially in the dark, with no moonlight, if you are out there all alone . . . it is so very easy to feel the spirits of the past, closing in around you, almost trying to pull you back in time . . . .

✳   ✳   ✳   ✳

If anyone would know about historical spirits, it is Mary Bray Wagner, site supervisor of the John Dickinson Plantation since 1988. Before arriving in Delaware, she had been an historical interpreter in Williamsburg, which, she added, has a number of ghostly legends. In fact, in one of the buildings where she hosted visitors many tourists said they felt a strong presence.

But, at the Delaware plantation, located in the area known as Jones Neck, she has had no unusual encounters.

"We're aware that legends do exist, but I checked with the staff, some of whom have been here for several years," Mary said, "and no one has seen anything of a ghostly nature.

"There are lots of noises and creaking," Mary said, adding that those are natural characteristics for a home built in 1740.

"The only time I'm afraid," she said, "is when I'm concerned that someone may have broken in. It's a very dark house, with very little electricity. You can't go from room to room and easily turn on the lights as you would in a modern home. So it's spooky in the sense that it's dark and shadowy, and most people are afraid of the dark."

Mary added, that, as historical interpreters, the guides and staff focus on facts that have been substantiated by newspapers, historical records and Dickinson family documents. The present caretakers' interest is in recreating daily life on the plantation in 18th-century Delaware. Legends and ghost tales are not subjects that the staff can verify or will discuss with any authority.

The site of the plantation is in the shadow of the Dover Air Force Base, about a half mile off Route 113 on Kitts Hummock Road.

Originally, the Dickinson family owned 5,000 acres in Kent County, with 3,500 of them stretching from the Delaware Bay to the area of the airbase. Today, the 18-acre site is maintained by the state, which opened the house to the public in 1956.

Spread throughout the grounds beyond the barn-like Visitors Center are the Mansion, Smoke House, Log'd Dwelling, Feed Barn, Stable, Corn Crib and Granary. Only one family member is known to be buried on the plantation, John's father, Samuel Dickinson, who settled the plantation and built the brick Georgian mansion in 1740.

Samuel's grave is well marked and surrounded by a brick wall.

Gloria Messina, who has been working as an interpreter at different state historical houses for 12 years, said she was unaware of any ghostly spirits, although their presence is questioned by visitors. But, she added, a lot of people had lived in the house. In addition to the Dickinsons, the home was rented to tenants for many years, up to the time the state took it over in 1952.

"We have a running joke," said Gloria. "We wonder what it was really like during those times. We say if we ever saw John or Samuel, we'd like to sit down and talk to them, to get a lot of things cleared up."

While not a ghost story, Gloria shared an interesting tale, documented through a recollection of a slave named Violet, who told the story to Sally, John Dickinson's daughter.

When John's father, Samuel, was quite ill, his favorite slave and servant, Pompey, died. Samuel directed the servants to move his bedroom to the first floor of the mansion, so he could see Pompey borne by fellow slaves who held a procession by the main house on their way to the burial grounds.

John Dickinson did not spend a majority of his life at the Jones Neck plantation. Born in 1732, he moved to Delaware from his boyhood home in Maryland in 1740, when he was 8, and stayed until 1750. He then spent time in England, studying law, and was a successful Philadelphia lawyer in 1760, when his father died.

By 1770, he married Mary Norris of Germantown, in Philadelphia. According to Gloria, he had an agreement with his tenants that whenever his family wanted to return to Kent County for a visit, there would be rooms readied for them.

A prominent figure in the Continental Congress, when the British invaded Philadelphia in 1777, he spent time at the plantation. And there was quite a bit of traveling back and forth during 1781, when he became president (or governor) of Delaware. Then, from 1782-1785, he agreed to serve as president of Pennsylvania.

Gloria described John as "quite a thinker." Despite the Quaker upbringing of his mother, and even though he refused to sign the Declaration of Independence, he served as a colonel in the Pennsylvania militia and saw action in the Battle of the Brandywine in September 1777.

Like his father, grandfather and great grandfather before him, John Dickinson was a slave owner. Messina said that records show he specifically bought slaves for the purpose of keeping families together. By 1786, he had freed all his slaves and hired some to work for him.

A fire in 1804 destroyed the interior of the brick portion of the mansion, and John took considerable care to rebuild the home. Today, visitors see an exterior built in 1740 and an interior that was reconstructed after the fire.

Gloria said the John Dickinson Plantation has national importance as a home of one of America's founding fathers. In addition, it offers visitors a view of how wealthy landowners, poor white tenant farmers and black slaves all lived during the late 18th and early 19th centuries.

Also, she stressed, John's birthplace in Maryland is gone. His home in Germantown no longer exists and his retirement home, at 8th and Market Streets in Wilmington has long ago been replaced.

"This mansion is the only remnant of where John Dickinson lived," said Gloria.

So perhaps, one might suggest, if the spirit of the Colonial statesman, who died on Feb. 14, 1808—who wrote against British oppression, who attempted to offer a voice of reason during the days of debate over independence, who was a Delaware delegate to the Constitutional Convention and who later wrote letters of advice to his friend President Thomas Jefferson—were seeking a comfortable, welcoming and familiar place to reside, it might certainly be his only remaining home, just southeast of Delaware's historic capital city.

Gloria smiled at the thought, then added, "Well, he certainly would be welcome, and he could give us a lot of answers."

The John Dickinson Plantation
INN*formation*

Inncidentally: The museum is operated by Delaware State Museums. Additional support is provided by The Friends of the John Dickinson Mansion Inc. It is located 6 miles south of Dover, on Kitts Hummock Road, just off Rt. 113, southeast of the Dover Air Force Base. Admission is free. Hours are 10 a.m.-3:30 p.m., Tuesdays-Saturdays; 1:30-4:30 p.m., Sundays. Closed Mondays and state holidays. Group tours are available, call to make arrangements. The Visitors Center, with a small gift shop, and the first floor of the Mansion are barrier free.

Innteresting notes: A 15-minute video in the Visitors Center gives an overview of the grounds and life during Dickinson's time. A large diorama offers a bird's-eye view of the plantation. Guided tours and informational booklets are offered. Interpreters provide interesting anecdotes and respond comfortably to questions. Archaeological work in the 1950s uncovered Samuel Dickinson's gravesite. The enclosure and simple headstone were erected during the restoration.

The Ghost is Inn: Possibly the Book Room, near the entrance hall, and the Master Bedroom, on the second floor. Also of interest is the dark Work Room, that occupies a lower level at the west end of the Mansion.

To get Inn touch: The John Dickinson Plantation, RD3, Box 257, Dover, DE 19901; telephone (302) 739-3277.

Chapter illustration courtesy of Delaware State Museums

KENT MANOR INN AND RESTAURANT · CIRCA 1820/1860

Alexander
of the
Kent Manor Inn

A delicate, octagonal cupola crowns the top of the Kent Manor Inn. The multi-paned, white latticed windows offer a magnificent view of the surrounding Eastern Shore, featuring hundreds of acres of lush farmland and miles of tranquil shoreline.

Today, inn visitors are able to stand at the exact spot from which Alexander Thompson, the building's former owner, kept an eye on his farmhands at work and viewed the progress of approaching ships nearly 150 years ago.

The original wing of the building was built in the 1820s on Kent Island land that was granted to Thomas Wetherall in 1651, only 17 years after Lord Calvert's arrival in Maryland.

Just prior to the Civil War, Alexander Thompson added the large central portion, with four rooms on both the first and second floors and five smaller ones on the third. The impressive addition featured Italian marble fireplaces, wide plank pine floors, hand-wrought oak woodwork on the stairway and sweeping walnut banisters.

Over the years, the home was used by subsequent owners as a private residence, a working farm and as a hotel. From 1904 to 1917, it was a summer hotel called Brightsworth Inn. Later, it operated under the name Pennysworth Farm.

In 1988, the property was purchased by Fred Williams, and since then he has operated and managed it with the help of his wife, Leslie Harper Williams. The inn, which highlights the historic property's 226 acres, contains 24 private guest rooms, two conference rooms and a three-star quality restaurant.

Leslie was seated in one of the main floor parlors, surrounded by period furniture, oriental carpeting and impressive antiques. In a relaxed manner, as if she was talking about friends and family, she shared slices of local history and her personal opinions about Alexander.

"He inherited the property from his mother," Leslie said. "He was married three times but had no children, and when he built the addition, it was referred to as 'Alexander's Folly' and 'Thompson's Folly.'

"There was no traffic coming by this area, other than a few passing boats, and only farmers lived nearby. Such a large house, even as an out-of-the-way inn, was not economically viable. I think of him as the area's Rhett Butler of the early 1800s. He entertained in this stately Southern-style plantation. He hosted grand parties, with orchestras playing in these rooms. Oftentimes, his guests stayed overnight when he held a ball."

When Leslie first arrived to work at the inn, a few descendants of some former owners asked her if she had seen Mr. Thompson riding up the driveway.

"They had lived here for several years," Leslie recalled, "and they said they would see Alexander riding up the driveway on his white steed."

While she has not seen the 19th-century gentleman ghost atop his horse, she did admit that she and some of the employees have had their share of interesting experiences.

Each night, Leslie explained, a member of the staff makes the rounds of each floor, locking every one of the 24 sleeping rooms that is not occupied by a guest. And each night, before she leaves, Leslie said she goes up and double checks that each door has been securely locked.

Frequently, finding a number of doors unsecured and open, she would make a note and leave it for the employee's attention the next morning.

"They would swear to me that they had closed the doors," Leslie said. "Eventually, they were afraid to go up to the third floor. One person swore that there was someone going behind her as she was walking down the hall, opening the doors she had locked.

She came flying down the stairs, announcing that she would never go back. And she still won't!"

A new employee, who had never heard any of the ghost stories, said she walked into Room 303 and saw a man sitting on the bed. She screamed and ran down the hall. Some of the other employees said, "You look like you've seen a ghost."

Apparently, she had.

The girl described the man she had seen as a farmer, wearing work boots, suspenders, a straw hat and smoking a pipe. She said she could even smell the tobacco.

"One thing we can be sure of," said Leslie, "it was not Alexander. He did not go out into the fields. He was a gentleman farmer, and he would go up into the cupola if he wanted to check on his workers."

Room 209, located in the original section of the home, was Alexander Thompson's master bedroom. Today, that room—which is tastefully decorated with two double beds, a television cabinet and has excellent views of the water—has been the site of a few noteworthy incidents.

During her first six months at the inn, Leslie stayed overnight in various unoccupied guest rooms. She said she would move from room to room, depending upon which were rented by guests. After a short time, she settled into Room 209.

"Sometimes, when I was watching TV," she said, "it would feel like someone was watching it with me. And someone or something would turn the TV on and off from time to time."

One morning, while alone and dressing in her room, Leslie had her back to the closed cabinet that held the television, which was not in use. Suddenly, she was startled by a man's voice loudly announcing: "Good morning!"

"It was a voice from the TV," Leslie recalled. "I was both startled and embarrassed. I shouted, 'Alexander! You aren't funny!' I think back on it and I know, intellectually, that this can't be true. But, instinctively, I know he was there watching me."

On another night in the same room, Leslie's daughter was visiting. They were watching television, and the set shut off. Neither woman had touched the set, and there was no remote control.

"I said, 'I guess Alexander thinks it's time we went to sleep.' I moved out of that room soon afterwards," Leslie added.

The only other incident in Room 209 was the complaint by guests who were annoyed by a tapping sound that had kept them awake all through their night's stay.

The innkeepers investigated and found there was no one in the rooms above on the third floor and no mechanical or physical explanation for the noises.

Lights turning on and off and table items being moved or disappearing occur frequently throughout the guest rooms and dining areas of the inn.

Leslie said she is careful to shut the lights off in every room when she locks up the building at the close of each evening. However, very frequently she sees lights on in various inn bedrooms when she starts to pull her car down the driveway.

"I've seen them on in Room 305, the Presidential Suite, and I know I turned them off," she said.

Did she go back in and turn them off?

"No! I wouldn't go back in, because I wouldn't go back up there alone. I even say to the workers, 'You come upstairs and watch me turn the lights out,' and it's happened a lot."

One of the more humorous events indirectly involving Alexander occurred in connection with a wedding.

The inn is a popular setting for bridal receptions. In addition to the Bridal Suite and overnight and restaurant facilities, the "Garden House," located behind the main building and adjacent to the swimming pool, can accommodate groups of up to 150.

"We were talking about the ghost to one bride when she came in to plan her wedding," said Leslie, "and she sent an invitation to the Kent Manor Inn addressed to Mr. Alexander Thompson, the ghost.

"She even had his room designated for one of her friends to stay in, and they were delighted with the whole thing. We saved the invitation for a long time."

One wonders what the owners and employees think of their unseen resident guests.

"I think we've kind of accepted this as something we've played upon," said Leslie. "Sometimes, I think we've tended to build more upon the ghost than there actually is. It's easy to attribute everything strange or unusual to Alexander and say, 'Oh. Alexander's up to no good again,' or 'Alexander's being mischievous.' "

As for guests, some request Alexander's room and others prefer not to risk the possibility of a phantom prankster.

"Some do ask for that room," said Leslie. "They explain that they've read about it in the magazine articles. But, we have just as many who say: 'Don't put me in the ghost room.' It's a perfectly beautiful room, but it has two double beds and most people prefer to sleep in a king-sized bed."

Explanations for Alexander's apparent decision to remain at the inn have not been discovered.

Leslie shared her feelings and explained that she has a very open mind regarding the unexplained. Perhaps, she said, Alexander— or whatever it is—happens to exist in a parallel dimension that, from time to time, crosses into the path of the current location and activities at the Kent Manor Inn.

"I believe some people are more sensitive to parallel events that may be happening," Leslie said. "I believe there are some people who can see the future or relive the events of the past. There is much more to this world than what we see, hear, feel or smell."

Kent Manor Inn and Restaurant

INN*formation*

Inncidentally: The inn offers nature paths and one-and-a-half miles of waterfront. It is accessible by land, sea (Thompson Creek) and air (Bay Bridge Airport). There are verandas off most of the first- and second-floor rooms. Shuttle service is available to the airport and nearby marinas. Public tennis courts and playgrounds are slightly over a mile away. Four Victorian dining rooms offer lunch and dinner daily and brunch on Sundays.

In 1991, the Kent Manor Inn was named the number one inn in the country, based on a random survey of guests by *The Inn Times* that listed the top 50 inns in America. The inn is listed in the Maryland Historical Sites Inventory.

Innteresting notes: On either side of the narrow stairway from the third floor to the cupola one can read the names and dates of visitors to Kent Manor Inn. Over the years, guests have signed their names and comments to the walls. Some areas have been preserved with special sealers. One entry, written nearly 90 years ago in fading pencil, reads: "Maurice Abels, 16 years of age, June 24, 1907."

The Ghost is Inn: Room 209, Alexander's master bedroom; also Room 303, where the farmer ghost appeared.

To get Inn touch: Kent Manor Inn and Restaurant, P.O. Box 291, Route 8 South, Kent Island, Stevensville, MD 21666; telephone, (410) 643-7716.

Chapter illustration courtesy of The Kent Manor Inn and Restaurant

Aunt Frances at
The River House Inn

Snow Hill, Maryland, settled in 1642, was named after a district of London. Because of its location on the Pocomoke River and access to the lower Chesapeake Bay, the town became a center for commerce, a site where lower Eastern Shore farmers could deliver and ship their goods to market.

The wealth and success of Snow Hill's 18th- and 19th-century entrepreneurs can still be seen in the stately homes that line streets bearing the names Green, Market, Federal, Martin, Collins, Washington and Church.

The town's Historic Walking Tour brochure provides information, a small map and the addresses of more than 50 "historically valuable homes" which are "very much a part of present Snow Hill."

More than 100 distinctive buildings of various styles still stand, and many of them were built before 1877. The town's architecture includes a wide range, from stately Federal to ornate Victorian.

However, out of all of the structures that catch a tourist's eye, only one, to our knowledge, has ever had a ghost deliver a roll of 19th-century wallpaper to the workers while the building was being restored.

The River House Inn's impressive facade faces East Market Street. Built about 1860, just before the start of the Civil War, the Gothic Revival structure has a wide, wrap-around porch. Its black shutters accent the inn's many windows, and several peaks and two chimneys cap the top of the house.

Two acres of rolling lawn that lead down to the Pocomoke River provide an appropriate frame to show off the preserved portrait of the home, owned for many years by the family of George Washington Purnell, a successful attorney.

Resident innkeepers Larry and Susanne Knudsen bought the building in March 1990. It had been occupied for many years by Mrs. Frances Thebaud, the last of the Purnell descendants who died in 1975.

Susanne, who also serves as Snow Hill's mayor, sat in the front parlor of the 135-year-old building and explained that the 13-room home had been in the same family for many years.

"Because of that, very little was done to change it from its original appearance," she explained. "The way you see it now is much as it was soon after it was built."

Susanne said there was a significant amount of restoration needed to bring the home up to modern standards, and she and her husband considered it important to maintain the essence of the original home.

One of the first chores was manually removing the old, faded, peeling wallpaper. In the twin parlor, at the front portion of the inn, a pattern formed by gold, Victorian wallpaper covered the ceiling.

"Like the paper in all the rooms, it had been on the walls for a hundred years," Susanne said. "The walls were cracked and the paper was soiled from years of smoking. We realized that all of the wallpaper had to come off, and we needed to do it quickly because we were planning to open in May."

The parlors were entirely empty, and the couple hired three men to help with the work. After a few days, Susanne came down the stairway early one morning, about seven o'clock, and there was a roll of wallpaper, in perfect condition, sitting on a small chair in the first floor hall.

"I asked my husband where it came from," she said, "and he had no idea. I asked the young men when they arrived for work. They didn't know. There was no place that it could have been hidden."

Susanne recalled placing it beside ripped pieces of the wallpaper the workers had been scraping off the ceiling, and it was an exact match.

"It was as if it had just been printed, brand new," she said. "It was just as though someone was saying: *Stop it! This is what belongs here!*"

61

Susanne contacted the former owner and asked if he had left any wallpaper behind.

The man replied that he had cleared out every inch of the house and there was no wallpaper, new or old, in the River House Inn when he left. In fact, he stressed, the house was totally empty.

Susanne paused from our conversation, walked to the deep bookcases beside the parlor's attractive faux marble fireplace, and pulled down the mysterious roll she had found that spring morning in 1990. Anyone could see, immediately, that the brittle paper was not manufactured recently and certainly could not be picked up at your local Sears wallpaper department.

Although this particular River House Inn mystery has never been solved, various theories have been proposed. And one, in particular, has become the explanation of record.

After examining a copy of the Purnell family tree, Susanne said she began referring to the mysterious wallpaper delivery person as Aunt Frances, who was a daughter of Elizabeth Purnell.

"We used to say, 'Aunt Frances is getting upset with all this redecorating.' But we don't hear from her any more, so I guess she's accepted what we've done and approves of it. I'm just happy that she's happy now."

Susanne said she never spent much time considering the existence of ghosts.

"I am sort of neutral about the whole subject," she explained. "Up until the time with the wallpaper, I had no personal experience. Since that happened, I've tried every which way to make sense of it. But there is no answer to the question as to where the wallpaper came from.

"That's the story," Susanne said. "It really was no major psychic encounter. And since we've had guests stay here, the cold feelings that I used to get on the stairway landing have stopped. I haven't had any more of those feelings since then. I've never made a big deal about the story. Sometimes, if the subject about ghosts comes up, we share this interesting anecdote. But we don't do it to scare people, and many of them find it quite interesting. My husband likes to haul the story out from time to time and amuse the guests."

The River House Inn
INN*formation*

Inncidentally: There are five guest rooms in the main house—the East, West, River and Colonial Rooms and the Third Floor Suite. The Little House, on the property, has three guest rooms—the Lilac and Garden Rooms and the Dover, a second floor suite. A carriage barn has been converted into the River Cottage, which also is available. The large back lawn that leads to the river accommodates weddings and private events. Larry is a licensed captain and, for a fee, can take guests on a river cruise aboard the inn's pontoon boat.

Innteresting notes: On the red painted wall, above the fireplace mantel in the Rear Parlor, is a square section of white featuring script writing that proclaims: *This room was papered April 30, 1890, by L. Edward Boehm and F. B. Russell. Artistic Paste Demolishers and Paint Slingers.* The two workmen had put the date and their signatures on the walls in every room in the house, and then papered them over. Susanne took photographs of each statement and decided to leave one on display. However, she said, referring to the less than ideal placement of the century-old message in the Rear Parlor: "I wish they had done it somewhere else. From a decorating standpoint, it's certainly not the best spot."

The Ghost is Inn: The Front Parlor, Entry Hall and Stairway Landing.

To get Inn touch: The River House Inn, 201 East Market Street, Snow Hill, MD 21863; telephone (410) 632-2722.

Chapter illustration courtesy of The River House Inn

J.J. at the Snow Hill Inn

Stroll along East Market Street in Snow Hill, Maryland, Worcester's County Seat, and you trace a pathway back into history. Uneven brick sidewalks, ornate, wrought iron fences and distinctive massive homes—that were built, in many cases, centuries ago—lead you to a time long gone but not yet forgotten.

During any season, and at any time of day, the pleasant setting encourages one to think of a less hectic, calmer era . . . when ladies carried parasols and wore bonnets and white gloves . . . when gentlemen tipped their silk top hats and sported handlebar mustaches . . . when friendly storekeepers used elastic garters to hold up their white, always white, French-cuffed shirtsleeves.

If you dare, take a few steps off the sidewalk, pass by the iron gate and climb the wooden steps of the Snow Hill Inn. As you enter through its doorway you may find yourself, not only within a remnant of the past, but in the midst of a living fragment of the unknown.

Displayed on the wall, between the lounge and restaurant areas, is a framed copy of an article that appeared in the *Baltimore Sun* on Aug. 14, 1993.

"The Ghost withInn," by staff writer Jean Marbella with photos by Mike Lutzky, gives visitors a hint of the building's real story in a feature article that highlights the exploits of the inn's most famous resident, a ghost affectionately referred to as "J.J."

Behind the bar in the Victorian Room lounge, an area that used to function as a bedroom, innkeeper Jennifer Carmean was not the least bit surprised when approached with the often-asked question: "Do you really have a ghost?"

"Oh. You mean J.J.," she replied, as if talking about a relative or close friend.

As she continued setting tables and cleaning the bar glasses, she casually recited a litany of events that have been attributed to the inn's ghost. These include turning lights on and off, locking doors, disturbing table settings and knocking on the walls of her bedroom.

Also, there are many times when Jennifer has had the feeling that "he" is standing behind her.

"I know there's a male figure standing behind me," she said, "and it's always in a doorway on the first floor, with his legs crossed. I can see the slight shape out of the corner of my eye. But when I turn, I don't see anything. But it very definitely is a male presence."

Kathy and Jim Washington bought the inn in 1990. The original section of the home had been built in the 1790s and was enlarged to its present size by 1850. In fact, one portion in the rear had served for a time as the Snow Hill Post Office.

The building's primary owner was Dr. John S. Aydelotte, a prominent member of the town.

Initially, the stories about ghosts were nothing more than interesting hearsay or passing gossip, said Kathy Washington. She recalled a story that she had heard about two construction workers who were remodeling the building several years before the Washingtons arrived on the scene.

The men were working in the Barrister Room, and they could not get the window open. They had tried everything possible to pry it loose and absolutely nothing worked. It was becoming an issue of both personal challenge and public humiliation.

Eventually, they gave up and were doing some other chores in the room when the window flew up on its own and the wind started blowing in.

According to Jim Washington, the story is that the men, who had been given free lodging in the building as part of the work arrangement, demanded to be put up someplace else. They would not stay overnight in the Snow Hill Inn.

"One lady," said Kathy, " comes in every other month for dinner and always wants to sit in the C Room, what we call the Sturgis Dining Room.

"The first time she came in, she told me, 'There's a presence here.' And she said she gets an incredible feeling when she comes here each time. That's how it's been. The guests bring the stories to us."

Over the course of their first six months at the inn, several guests shared unexpected stories with the new owners.

A lady awoke one night and saw a figure walking across the foot of the bed and pass into the bathroom. At first, Kathy said, the woman thought it was her husband. But then she turned and saw her husband was still asleep beside her.

"The next morning at breakfast," Jim said, "the guest shared her story with us and added, 'You all have a ghost here.' "

Kathy said she never was quite sure of the spirit's existence, mainly because she had never seen the ghost herself. She also said, as the owners, they never went out of their way to share their unusual experiences.

But, one of their guests did.

A Towson, Maryland, attorney and her 12-year-old son had an experience while staying in the Wicker Room in June 1993.

According to Kathy and the *Sun* newspaper article, the boy was in the bathroom. When he turned around, he saw a young man, who appeared to be in his early twenties, standing across the room. And when he looked again, there was no one there. The boy knew nothing about any other unusual ghostly experiences in the inn.

The woman contacted *The Baltimore Sun*, and they published the article that hangs on the wall.

Kathy said she isn't bothered by the events associated with J.J., and she has started to get a better sense of his preferences.

"He likes lights," she said. "Candles are lit by themselves. In the Sturgis Room we don't light the candles for lunch. We will go in at 11 in the morning and they are lit. Or you'll walk in and notice the strong smell of smoke, from out of nowhere. Then, 15 minutes later, it's gone. No smoke, no odor."

Perhaps the oddest and funniest incident associated with the ghost was the locked restroom door in the Victorian Lounge.

One evening the small bar was filled with regulars. Eventually, one of the customers went to the restroom door, turned and pulled on the doorknob and it would not open.

Apparently, he thought, it was occupied.

Time went by and others had to use the facilities. But no one had exited from the restroom.

"We sat here for over an hour," said Kathy, laughing as she recalled the incident. "And we thought, if somebody is in there, my God, they're in there for a long time."

After several knocks and shouts to awaken whomever might have fallen asleep in the "john," there was still no response. Without too much prodding, the regulars got their tools out and took the locked door off its hinges.

When they peered into the small room, that has no other exit door or window, it was empty. Also, the door had not been secured by the simple lock on the doorknob. It had been locked by the sliding deadbolt. But, Kathy said, to make the deadbolt operate, one has to apply significant effort to forcefully lift the door so the bolt can slide across to secure it properly.

And, that had been accomplished by someone, or something, that was nowhere to be found.

"They really tried to laugh it off," said Kathy, "but that night we got a few of them really thinking: *What's going on here?*"

Some think they may know the identity of the phantom who prowls the restaurant and guest rooms of the Snow Hill Inn. They have offered the name of William J. Aydelotte as their candidate.

According to Baltimore newspaper reports printed in December 1904, the 22-year-old student at the Maryland School of Pharmacy in Baltimore was depressed over fear that he would fail an examination. In a note that was found in his rooming house, he wrote to his father stating it is "useless to keep me at school. . . . "

The younger Aydelotte was discovered the next day, groaning and bleeding profusely from several self-inflicted gashes across his throat. He died in the hospital and his body was brought back to Snow Hill for burial.

If J.J. is the ghost of Snow Hill Inn, it has been 91 years since his despondent departure from the earthly world.

No one knows for what specific reasons he has returned, or if, in fact, he has ever really left his home on East Market Street. Some believe that certain spirits will make their presence known only when they feel most comfortable with their surroundings.

If so, the present owners of Snow Hill Inn may well consider J.J.'s antics as ghostly signals that he considers them welcome in his family's home, and that he intends to remain with the new occupants for a very long time.

"It doesn't scare me. I don't think he's here to hurt us," Kathy said. "I believe he's here, and he's friendly. But I want to see him. I never have. It seems that the ones who are leery of ghosts are the ones who are experiencing this.

"The closest I got was when I saw someone go out the back kitchen door. I know it wasn't a person, or a cat or a dog or mouse. There was no one else inside here with me that day. But I know I saw it, something. I was so close. I think maybe I am trying too hard."

Snow Hill Inn
INN*formation*

Inncidentally: The house is described as a 19th-century Country Victorian. There are three guest rooms with private baths, one with a working fireplace. The restaurant accommodates up to 70 diners. The lounge is open seven days a week. Dinner is served Wednesdays through Sundays and lunch is available Mondays through Fridays.

Innteresting notes: Kathy said one cleaning lady said she wouldn't work alone in the inn when the ghost was about. She also swore that the ghost had come back because there was money hidden somewhere in the inn. "Where there's a haunt, there's money," the elderly cleaning lady said. "Well," Kathy replied, "you better start cleaning deeper."

The Ghost is Inn: The Victorian Lounge and Restroom, Barrister Room, Wicker Room and the Sturgis Dining Room.

To get Inn touch: Snow Hill Inn, 104 East Market Street, Snow Hill, MD 21863; telephone (410) 632-2102.

Chapter illustration courtesy of Snow Hill Inn

Family and Friends
at Rockwood Museum

To view Rockwood for the first time is both an eerie and exciting experience.

As you pass through the imposing gates and travel up the winding, forested drive, a clearing appears on the left, making it possible to snatch your first glimpse of the mansion and manicured gardens.

Initially, the words elegant, massive, noble, wealthy and grand come to mind. But as you approach the Rural Gothic graystone structure, the idea *haunted* arrives, accompanied by several exclamation points.

Standing in the spacious Entrance Hall, however, all thoughts of spirits temporarily disappear, for your senses are both captured and intrigued by the elegant and impressive interior. Eyes automatically shift upward and travel from side to side, scanning the grand stairway, formal paintings and fine antiques.

Rockwood Museum, in northern Delaware, is located very close to Interstate 95. But you feel far removed from 20th-century traffic and bedlam. With little effort, you can easily allow yourself to imagine that you've been transported to a calmer, more refined age.

The large manor house was the home of Joseph Shipley, a merchant banker and descendant of a founder of Wilmington. Joseph made his fortune in England during the first half of the 19th century.

70

In 1854, when he moved into his newly built estate, Shipley's secluded country home consisted of more than 300 acres, including the 1,100 trees and shrubs he had imported for his private gardens. The house had the most modern conveniences of the time, including a central heating system and a bathroom with an interior water closet.

Additions made by Joseph and his descendants increased the manor house to its present size, totaling more than 50 rooms. Other structures on the estate include a stable, carriage house, gardener's cottage, ice house and porter's lodge, many of which remain in use.

After ownership passed through a succession of heirs, the last family member, Nancy Sellers Hargraves, died in 1972, leaving instructions that the house and land be given to a charitable organization.

In 1974, the Delaware Court of Chancery deeded Rockwood to New Castle County as a museum and reception center. After some renovations, the museum was formally opened to the public on Sept. 23, 1976.

✣　　✣　　✣　　✣

Jack Braunlein, director of Rockwood Museum, has been in that position since 1983. In his office, located in the wing built in 1912 and overlooking the sweeping lawn and stately trees, he discussed some unusual incidents that he and others have experienced.

"I was aware of the reputation of Rockwood," he said, quite calmly, "and aware that some believed there was something unusual going on here. But I'm a ghost agnostic. I tend to feel that there are events that are influenced by our sense of imagination. But, I must admit, there are a number of happenings that have occurred here that cause one to leave the door open."

It was veteran volunteer Eleanor Merrill who recalled an early experience involving her and Jack.

She was working in the gift shop, not far from the manor house, one Saturday. The museum was closed for some renovations and Jack had been working alone in the building. He locked the doors, went to Eleanor's building, and suggested that she go into the main house's kitchen and have lunch while he watched the shop.

"He gave me his keys, and I unlocked the door and went into the house," she said. "I immediately heard footsteps upstairs, coming from the office area. They were moving at a fast pace, in what my mother would have called sensible heels, not dress high heels. I never saw anybody. All I heard were the footsteps, and they were hurrying, not running, across the second floor of the building.

"They were so real. I did not imagine it, and no one will ever convince me that what I heard did not happen."

Eleanor said she became uneasy and left quickly. But before she returned to the gift shop, she walked around the building, looking in the windows to see if anyone was about.

When she saw Jack, she asked if anyone else was in the main house. When he replied no, she told him what had happened.

"He looked surprised," Eleanor said. "There was another man in the gift shop at the time, and the two of them checked all the doors and windows. And they found absolutely nothing. But I was still concerned, and still positive about what I heard."

Yvonne Palmer, another volunteer, heard footsteps coming from the same second floor hall when she and a friend were preparing for a luncheon in the manor house one Saturday morning. As in Eleanor's case, after investigating, the two women found no one else in the building.

Smiling at the footsteps stories, Jack recalled a few of his own experiences.

One night, working late in his office, the radio came on.

"I don't know why or how," he said. "It was the kind of radio that you have to twist the knob to operate. There's probably some good explanation. But, I just turned the radio off and left immediately. I just didn't want to cope with it."

After those incidents, and having heard other stories, Jack's sensitivity to the unexplained had been activated. One evening, he heard a steady tapping. He got up several times to search for the cause, but could not determine the source.

Admittedly getting nervous, he stood up, preparing for whatever might enter the office. Then, he realized the steady sound was the result of tree droppings falling on the roof above.

At least this one "unusual" incident was resolved logically, he said, laughing.

But, it seems that many other tales of Rockwood conclude with a series of large-sized question marks.

Suzie is a dedicated volunteer who has been a guide at the museum almost since it opened. She was eager to share the events that greeted her on a cold, icy slick December night, when she and her husband arrived at Rockwood to prepare the rooms for a scheduled candlelight tour.

While making final arrangements for the guests, Suzie heard a strange sound coming from the servants' stairway that led to the main floor kitchen area. Investigating, she and her husband saw a stream of water flowing down the stairs.

Tracing the source of the wet, moving trail, they arrived in the second floor hallway. More water was flowing from the next stairway that lead to the third floor servants' quarters.

Climbing to that level to find the source, the couple discovered that the tub faucets of the servants' bathroom had been turned on, full force.

The drain could not accommodate the flow, and the tub was filled, sending a steady trail of water to the ground level two floors below.

"It didn't make any sense," Suzie said. "I had been there all day. There was no reason to turn on the faucets as no one occupied the house."

The next day, Suzie returned to prepare for another candlelight tour.

"The water was on again, in the same place," she said. "It wasn't flowing over this time. It was more of a slow trickle, but not a leaky dripping. It definitely had been turned on. Someone had to have twisted those faucets. It didn't happen on its own."

One of Jack's strangest tales involves the security guard who responded to a call late one evening.

"He was in the Entrance Hall and heard footsteps upstairs," Jack said. "After checking the building completely and finding nothing, he came back down into the hall. That's when he noticed that one of the family photographs, which had been upright when he had come in, was turned face down."

Whose picture was it?

"Mrs. Hargraves," Jack said, "the last family descendant who lived here and the person who had left the home to a charitable organization." Pausing, and offering a slight smile, Jack added, "The guard left immediately."

Suzie recalled a housekeeper companion of Mrs. Hargraves saying that the last owner would not stay in the house alone.

"According to her housekeeper," Suzie added, "Mrs. Hargraves was alone one night, when her husband was away. She later said she heard all kinds of things, all night long, walking around. Mrs. Hargraves locked herself in her bedroom and pushed chairs up against the door and wouldn't come out."

Another incident involved Buttercup, a former servant who worked for Mrs. Hargraves at Rockwood, who heard a tapping sound coming from upstairs. When she climbed the stairs to investigate, Buttercup said she saw an elderly lady, bent over and walking very slowly with a cane.

The woman entered the North Bedroom and disappeared.

When Buttercup told Mistress Hargraves about the incident, the owner confirmed there was no guest in the home. Later, the two women looked through a family photograph album, and Buttercup identified a picture of the unscheduled guest with the tapping cane.

On another evening, a former curator was at work in the office. Her husband and a friend were playing a game, waiting for her to finish, when an unexpected knock on the door sent everyone downstairs to investigate.

There was no one outside, but all confirm they had heard a distinct knocking sound.

When the trio returned to the second floor office area, they noticed a table in the Monte Carlo Room, a former servants area near the present day staff offices.

There had been a display of old playing cards, dealt out as if for a game of Whist, on one of the tables.

The cards, which had been accurately arranged for tour visitors, had been disturbed and rearranged while the three perplexed searchers had been downstairs, responding to the phantom's knocking.

Suzie was eager to share the interesting visit of three female psychics.

"They said they knew we were open and asked permission to come through the building," Suzie recalled. "It was in the early days, when we first opened, and we were happy to have visitors."

While walking through, the women offered several comments, and one psychic said there was someone in the staff area. She described him as a man in a wheelchair who was lost.

Suzie said the psychic explained that the man was not angry or upset, only lost.

At first, the comments didn't make sense. But, Suzie explained, "Joseph Shipley, the builder, was in a wheelchair the last year of his life. And, if it was Joseph, he would have been lost because he died in 1867. The wing where the psychic saw the man wasn't built until 1912. So, of course, he was lost and didn't understand where he was."

A second psychic described the presence of a servant who was wearing glasses that pinched onto the top of her nose.

"That," Suzie said, "was Annie. We have a picture of her. She worked for Mary Bringhurst."

Suzie, still an active volunteer and member of the Friends of Rockwood, said she and others have experienced the sounds of footsteps, knocking and doors opening and closing.

"Absolutely, there is a presence here," Suzie said. "I think there are a few. I wouldn't be surprised if Joseph Shipley is here, as well as other members of the family and their servants.

"This is a fascinating place. I've never been afraid, ever. There is never a sense that there is anything nasty or harmful here. All of the people who lived in Rockwood thought it was a very important home. Now that it's being preserved, I think they're pleased with what is happening."

Jack Braunlein agreed that much has occurred at Rockwood over the years to enhance its mission, that of preserving and interpreting an important era of American history.

"While, of course, we get questions about ghosts," he said, "we try to emphasize the social history, the family members and servants who both lived and worked here. We try to create what it was like on a country estate in Delaware from 1890-1920. As visitors tour the rooms, we want them to get the impression that the family has just gone out and will be back later."

Creating that atmosphere is possible since all of the family furnishings, antiques, clothing, documents and correspondence accompanied the transfer of the estate to New Castle County. Today, visitors are able to view English, American and Continental furniture from the 17th, 18th and early 19th centuries, along with portraits of many generations of Shipley and Bringhurst family members.

Jack said individual guides respond to ghost-related questions in whatever manner they feel comfortable.

"There is a degree of mystery associated with Rockwood," he admitted. "Part of this interest is created by the Gothic architecture of the house itself. I think that naturally brings with it a sense of mystery.

"At night, it is absolutely pitch black out here. It's a perfect setting to let your imagination go wild. Being an old house, it creaks and groans on the inside, and outside. In the woods, you hear all types of movement and sounds. All that would get anyone thinking about what might be out there."

Or, even perhaps, what might be inside?

Rockwood Museum
INN*formation*

INNcidentally: The museum is owned and operated by the New Castle County Department of Parks and Recreation. Guided tours are offered 11 a.m.-4 p.m. (last tour begins at 3 p.m.), Tuesdays through Saturdays (open Sundays, March through December). It is closed on major holidays. Groups of 10 or more must make reservations in advance. Tours are appropriate for all age levels, including school groups. Special tours are available for individuals with disabilities. Admission is $5 for adults; $4 for senior citizens; and $2 for children (5-16).

INNteresting notes: Six acres of elegant gardens surround the immediate area around the manor house. Rooms are filled with furniture, antiques, portraits and decorative collectibles. Tours last approximately one hour. Nearly 20,000 visitors tour Rockwood each year, with thousands attending the annual Rockwood Ice Cream Festival each July. Special events and a concert series are scheduled during the year. The building may be rented for private functions, meetings and luncheons. Catering is available.

The Ghost is Inn: Entrance Hall, Second Floor Hallway, Monte Carlo Room, North Bedroom and Servants' Bathroom (third floor).

To get Inn touch: Rockwood Museum, 610 Shipley Road, Wilmington, DE 19809; telephone, (302) 761-4340.

Chapter illustration courtesy of Art by Architects, Delaware Society of Architects and the Rockwood Museum

Concert by Candlelight

I had just completed a session of stories at the Sea Witch Inn. The beautifully restored Victorian home is nestled on the banks of the Chesapeake and Delaware Canal, in the picturesque town of Chesapeake City, Maryland, about halfway between Philadelphia and Baltimore.

The presentation had gone quite well. The intimate audience that had gathered in the dimly lit parlor was especially warm and responsive on that cold winter night.

After exchanging pleasantries following the program, I retired to the quaint, dark paneled sitting room, which was dominated by a turn-of-the-century carved mahogany bar. With the compliments of the owner, I was enjoying a steaming cup of Irish coffee when a short rotund gentleman approached and requested a few moments of my time.

I nodded and he pushed over a wing backed chair. Smiling, he plopped his ample frame into the cushions and we passed more than an hour in interesting conversation.

He was a guest at the inn and offered a Cheshire cat grin as he told me he was very familiar with the haunted Federal mansion I had described. It overlooked the top of the Chesapeake Bay in nearby Port Deposit. The setting had been the topic of one of my real-life ghost stories—the evening's theme.

As very late evening approached very early morning—and the innkeeper was giving us definite signals by rattling his bar glasses a bit more loudly than usual—I began to make my excuses to leave. It was then that the well-spoken fellow, shaped very much

like the mayor of Munchkin City in *The Wizard of Oz*, produced a
sealed envelope.

"What are you doing on the eve of Father's Day?" he asked.

I pulled out my calendar, checked and said I was available.

"Very fine," said my new friend, whose name I learned was
Woitek. "Here's $200 as a retainer for a one-hour session of real-
life ghosts and horror, your very best."

He handed me the paper, with my name written in sweeping
script across the top.

Naturally, I accepted the proposal. After all, the demand on
that June evening wasn't going to be anything like Halloween.

"And," he added, "there's an additional $200 at the end of the
evening, and a possible bonus if they like you."

Before I could ask any questions about the audience and setting, he got up to leave, adding that everything I needed to know
was included in the envelope.

I shook his hand, added my thanks and watched him clutch
the wooden railing as he slowly ascended the carpeted stairs
toward his room.

Later that night, when I arrived home, I opened my instructions,
depositing the two crisp one-hundred-dollar bills in my pocket.

According to what I read, it was going to be a full night.

I was to be dressed in formal attire and would be picked up
by limousine at the front door of the Sea Witch Inn. The vehicle
would take me to the concert site and provide for my return early
the next morning.

The only stipulation: I was to deliver a set of adult tales to
chill the bone.

No problem, I told myself. Making horror live was my life.

Throughout the spring, I collected and perfected a series of
real blood curdlers. After trying them out on my most critical
friends, I could tell by their shivering reactions that I was ready.

At 6 p.m. on Father's Day eve, I descended the stairs from the
porch of the Sea Witch Inn and stepped into the back of the black
Cadillac where Woitek awaited me. An early 1970s model, it
reminded me of a funeral parlor limo, featuring small fins and
tastefully accented with genuine, made-in-America chrome.

Woitek shook my hand and we passed the travel time in chat-
ter, mainly about the distant points he had traveled and the many

storytellers he had heard—in such diverse places as Ireland, India, Poland and Brazil.

The darkened windows did not allow me to see where we were going, but it didn't really matter. After all, I didn't have to drive.

Eventually, when I checked my watch I was amazed. It was approaching eight o'clock.

"What time do I go on?" I asked.

"When we arrive," Woitek replied.

"When will that be?" I asked.

"When we get there," he said, the Cheshire smile had returned.

"Where are we going?"

"To a nice place, a quiet theater in a section of Baltimore."

"How many do you expect in the audience?" I wondered.

"That depends on how much they like you."

Much of this made little sense. But rather than try to sort out the puzzle, I settled back and mulled over the general details of my concert selections.

Shortly before nine the car came to a stop.

Woitek and I stepped out onto the curb and stood beneath the bare, damaged marquee of a long-closed, neighborhood movie theater.

Obviously built in the 1930s, several small, hand-carved gargoyles and laughing gnomes looked down on us as we stood in the quiet darkness of the empty street.

Woitek waved his arm toward the old-fashioned entrance and pushed open the heavy metal door.

The lobby was dark, but we followed a glow that could be seen in a distant portion of the building. As we turned the corner on the frayed, purple carpeting, we stood in the mirrored rear foyer of a once magnificent vaudeville and movie house.

Its stage and aisles were lit by hundreds of blazing candles.

I could see the yellow glow in the area, slightly ahead, that was illuminated by candlelight. But I noticed no one in the seats.

"What's going . . . ." I never finished the question.

Woitek put his finger to his lips, signaling silence.

In the tattered rear vestibule, beside a wall adorned with heavy brocade draperies, he pulled me aside and whispered: "Few tellers have performed for this evening's select gathering of distinguished guests. I selected you very carefully. No matter what happens, finish the session, all of your tales. No matter what happens, do not leave the stage until the very end."

I nodded.

"I will be waiting for you afterwards. If they like you, you will know it . . . . It's time for you to begin. Good luck."

My feet seemed to float above the shabby, violet-carpeted aisle as I covered the distance from the foyer to the stage.

There was no one in the building. No person I could see.

I remember thinking at the time that there might be a few people in the dark corners where the light from the candles didn't reach, but I wasn't sure.

My mind was torn between searching for answers to the puzzle and concentrating on my program. What a sweet deal this arrangement had seemed. Now, what a strange situation I was in. And I didn't even know where I was.

Reaching the front of the building, I turned.

Woitek stood alone in the center of the main aisle, his short, round figure distorted by the odd glow.

He introduced me. There was no need for a microphone. His jovial voice bounced off the flying buttresses that were sweeping toward the naked ladies who were painted on the ceilings. Several of them were looking down on me and the empty hall. I wondered what was holding them up, noticing there were quite a few tainted cherubs on all sides of the ornate chandelier medallions.

"LADIES AND GENTLEMEN!

"MEMBERS AND GUESTS. . .

"Tonight's storyteller has arrived!

"With no further delay. . . .

"LET THE CONCERT BEGIN!!!"

No applause.

Nothing.

The stone dead silence was broken only by the periodic soft crackling of hundreds of candle wicks.

In the flickering natural light of late evening, in an entertainment hall of another age, I began . . . .

"On a ragged cliff, at the edge of a ridge overlooking the Susquehanna River, stands the remnants of a crumbling, turreted mansion. Built by the sweat of slaves in another time, it remains a symbol of an earlier age, a relic of the late 1700s.

"But while its owners have passed on, and slavery has long ago been abolished, and eight-lane highways pass through its fields that once grew tobacco and grain, some believe that many of the slaves have remained. With their bodies buried in a deep pit in the dirt-floored cellar, their disturbed souls continue to crawl out at night to roam at will along the cliffs and wharf of Port Deposit."

My eyes moved around the room—I scanned the empty aisles, the vacant seats. I looked back and forth as I spoke—at where there should have been listeners. Soon, the more I talked, the more figures I began to see. Not in the front rows, but in the rear seats and in the shadowy corners of the building.

The lighting was horrible, it's low level distorting my view. I couldn't make out the figures' faces. They seemed to be only soft, mask like images.

The unusual glow, resulting from the flickering candles, made it appear as if some in the audience were moving, floating, almost hovering around the seats.

At the end of my first story, the theater was about a quarter full. I did not see them come in, but they were there. I received no applause, but instead a different intensity of glow came from each person as he or she appeared.

The second tale, about the dead sea captain who came back and murdered his unfaithful wife and her lover, was quite popular, for it increased the size of the audience to fill more than half the seats. Still, the first three rows were totally empty, and much of the front of the building remained bare of listeners.

A somewhat humorous presentation about the reaction of the living to ghostly visits was well received. And, for the first time, I saw a few front row center patrons seemingly come to life.

It was then, in the midst of that tale, that I realized my audience was not of this world, not a warm, living, breathing congregation.

I was speaking to a social gathering for the dead.

Somehow I maintained my poise and completed the concert. After all, I reasoned, the audience seemed appreciative enough, the money as good. Besides, they deserved to be entertained, especially since many of their bizarre plights had served as the basis for grisly tales that supported my career.

The last story, about the vampire Christmas feast where small, lost children were shared among the dead as holiday gifts, grabbed the attention of those who must have reserved the best seats in the house.

While telling this insensitive story of blood letting and gore, I wondered if there was an order of importance—since the vampires or the undead were seated up front, the witches concentrated in the middle and the zombies and ghosts sat to the rear and the sides of the theater.

I'd have to ask Woitek about that, I tried to remind myself.

It was a bit odd to hear no applause or "normal" reaction. But the glow around so many of the audience, and their faint images bobbing up and down, were to serve as my reward—plus the balance and decent monetary bonus I received from my host.

There was no after-the-show reception, no pressing of the flesh in the lobby. But the final walk up the aisle to the lobby and limousine was electric. I felt an amazing rush as the candlelight mixed with hundreds of individual ghostly auras.

In the Caddy, Woitek was beaming. We both smoked cigars on the return ride.

I listened with interest as Woitek explained that the dead had their own holiday celebrations. With them, money was no problem, and he could get the best entertainment, whether it be musicians, actors, dancers or storytellers.

"You'd be surprised at the name acts that I've hired," Woitek said, proudly puffing away. "You're in good company, kid."

The tough part, he said, was finding someone who could handle the strange, bizarre settings.

"You know," he said, pointing his cigar like a piece of dark chalk, "It's funny. You storytellers all shoot off a good yarn about the ghosts and the ghoulies, but very few of you have the ability to handle the real thing. When we find one who can, like you, we put them on the top of our entertainment list and we try to use them often. You did real good job tonight, pal."

As he said this, he produced another envelope.

"I'm not ready to move you up to Halloween or New Year's Eve or Valentine's Day yet. They're our marquee gigs. But be ready for Veteran's Day eve. Need a bunch of good war stories—from the ghost's point of view, of course," he smiled.

"Of course," I replied, offering my own newly acquired, Woitek-Cheshire smile.

That was four years ago.

Since that tryout night in Baltimore, I've presented shows on the eve of Canada's National Holiday in Quebec, at a July Fourth men's club party in Philadelphia for several signers of the Declaration of Independence, for Will Rogers and his friends during the humorist's annual festival in Oklahoma and at a private Valentines Day party, that was attended by Edgar Allan Poe, Vincent Price and Bela Lugosi, in a luxury hotel overlooking Baltimore's Inner Harbor.

A few spirit fans have even passed along their experiences through Woitek, and portions of their material have found their way into my stories.

To some, this whole scenario might sound a bit strange, and I admit it did take a little getting used to. But an attentive, well-paying, steady, captive audience, with all the time in the world, is hard to find.

But there was a nagging concern.

One evening, over dinner at a private university club in downtown Baltimore, I asked Woitek what would happen if his clients didn't like a presentation.

He paused, leaned over and said, "All they want is authentic, fresh material. Stuff that is thoroughly researched and prepared well. No rehashed crap.

"We had this woman once," he said, shaking his head. "She certainly didn't do her homework, thought she'd be clever and tried to redo the story of Lizzie Borden. You know, the kid who gave her mother 40 whacks and then turned around and snuffed out the old man, too."

"Yeah, I know," I explained. "So what was the problem?"

"Well, she had, what she thought, was this great idea to do a comedy routine at Lizzie's expense. Present the story with a humorous slant.

"But, surprise!

"Guess who was in the audience that night? Right! Liz, herself. And our original hatchet swinger was very insulted, embarrassed in fact. Things did not go well after that."

"So what happened to the teller? Did you fire her?"

My patron leaned back in his chair and then took a drag on his Cuban cigar.

"No, nothing like that," he said, leaving me hanging.

"What then?" I pressed.

That's when Woitek puffed out his chest and flashed his gleaming ivories, "Liz . . . and several of her closest friends, *invited* that creative lady to become a permanent member of the audience."

—Ed Okonowicz

About the Author

*E*d Okonowicz, a Delaware native, is a freelance writer for local newspapers and magazines. Many of his feature articles have been about ghosts and spirits throughout the Delmarva Peninsula. He is employed as an editor and writer at the University of Delaware, where he earned a bachelor's degree in education and a master's degree in communication.

Also a professional storyteller, Ed is a member of the National Storytelling Association and several regional storytelling organizations. He presents programs at country inns, retirement homes, schools, libraries, public events, private gatherings, birthday parties, Elderhostels and theaters in the mid-Atlantic region.

He specializes in local legends and folklore of the Delaware and Chesapeake Bays, as well as topics related to the Eastern Shore of Maryland. He also writes and tells city stories, many based on his youth growing up in his family's beer garden–Adolph's Cafe–in Wilmington. He tells tales about the unusual characters each of us meet in our everyday lives.

Ed presents beginning storytelling courses and also writing workshops based on his book *How to Conduct an Interview and Write an Original Story*.

About the Artist

*K*athleen Burgoon Okonowicz, a watercolor artist and illustrator, is originally from Greenbelt, Maryland. She studied art in high school and college, and began focusing on realism and detail more recently under Geraldine McKeown. She enjoys taking things of the past and preserving them in her paintings.

Her first full-color, limited-edition print, *Special Places*, was released in January 1995. The painting features a stately stairway near the Brandywine River in Wilmington, Delaware.

A graduate of Salisbury State University, Kathleen earned her master's degree in professional writing from Towson State University. She is currently a marketing analyst at the International Reading Association in Newark, Delaware.

The couple resides in Fair Hill, Md.

Coming

Spring 1996

Possessed Possessions:
Haunted Antiques, Furniture and Collectibles
by Ed Okonowicz

True tales of unusual events associated with objects that certainly seem to have a *spirit* of their own!

Dare to peek into our
cobwebbed cabinet of curios and meet. . .

The Troubled Doll

Jonathan's Haunted Chair

Goblins in the Mirror

Sydney's Talking Candlestick

Don't Open the Trunk

Grandfather's Dining Room Set

The Anniversary Ring

The Haunted Headboard

and more

I am constantly looking for more stories. If you have had a ghostly experience with an object or if you know of a haunted site that is accessible to the public, I would appreciate hearing from you. Please use the form on Page 90.

Attractions

To order additional volumes, or to share an encounter or tale

To submit your personal experience for consideration, to purchase additional books or to be placed on our mailing list, please complete the form below.

Name _____

Address _____

City _____ State _____

Zip Code _____

Phone Numbers ( ) _____ ( ) _____
                     Day   Evening

_____I would like to be placed on the mailing list to receive the free *Spirits Speaks* newsletter and information of future volumes.

_____I have an experience I would like to share. Please call me. (Each person who sends in a submission will be contacted. If your story is used, you will receive a free copy of the volume in which your experience appears.)

I would like to order the following books:

Quantity	Title	Price	Total
	Pulling Back the Curtain, Vol. 1	$8.95	
	Opening the Door, Vol. II	$8.95	
	Welcome Inn, Vol. III	$8.95	
	Stairway over the Brandywine, A Love Story	$5.00	
		Shipping	
		Total	
Please include $1.50 postage for the first book, and 50 cents for each additional book.			

Send to: Ed Okonowicz
1386 Fair Hill Lane
Elkton, MD 21921